Praise for *Text Messages*

"Yassin 'Narcy' Alsalman is a one-of-a-kind artist. He is transcendental, he is pop, he is the Muslim, he is the poet. Through his questioning of the tides of time, and the world's disregard of the Arab, he writes lyrics as anthem, providing a source material for a part of the world that is so often misunderstood and forgotten. This book is exciting in its futurity. It is punchy in its enthusiasm. I am grateful for this book's aliveness."

—**Fariha Róisín**, author, *How To Cure a Ghost*

"Yassin Alsalman's writing weaves through the epic struggles of people to get free, enduring and resisting brutality, dictatorship, war, and occupation. As a hip-hop artist, he was forged in the rubble of 9/11 and the ensuing war against Muslims, emerging as one of the most creative and sharp artists chronicling the crimes of the powerful and giving voice to people's uprisings. *Text Messages* is a potent book rooted in the poetry and art of Alsalman's Iraqi ancestors, translated in a global language for the urgency of the times in which we now live."

—**Jeremy Scahill**, co-founder of *The Intercept*
and author of *Blackwater* and *Dirty Wars*

"Yassin Alsalman possesses one of the most important voices in the world, and *Text Messages* could not be more timely or more necessary of a read. On paper, this Muslim teacher who raps should not be a success, but because of the beauty of his words and the pureness of his heart, he wins despite the massive odds against him. Narcy makes me feel heard, he gives me life. I am proud to be his friend and his peer."

—Talib Kweli

"Narcy's voice cuts through the rubble piled high in the wake of Amerikkka's 'War on Terror,' a true testament to hip-hop's intersectional revolutionary power and an unapologetic representation of the Muslim world in the 21st century's most ubiquitous art form."

—Vic Mensa

"Passion, pain, anger, hope, and swagger. Yassin is a man from the future. Narcy beautifully captures the chaotic multitudes of being a brown diaspora kid living through the war on terror in the technology age. Text Messages is an ambitious and bold time capsule capturing the insane times we're living through. Poems, barbs, and bars—take a bow, Yassin, you've made a classic."

—Hasan Minhaj

TEXT
MESSAGES
or How I Found Myself Time Travelling

Yassin "Narcy" Alsalman

Haymarket Books
Chicago, Illinois

Printed and bound in Canada

Published by Roseway Publishing
an imprint of Fernwood Publishing
32 Oceanvista Lane, Black Point, Nova Scotia, B0J 1B0
and 748 Broadway Avenue, Winnipeg, Manitoba, R3G 0X3
www.fernwoodpublishing.ca/roseway

Fernwood Publishing Company Limited gratefully acknowledges the financial support of the Government of Canada through the Canada Book Fund, the Canada Council for the Arts, the Province of Nova Scotia and the Province of Manitoba for our publishing program.

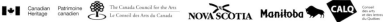

Library and Archives Canada Cataloguing in Publication.
Title: Text messages : or how I found myself time travelling / Yassin "Narcy" Alsalman.
Names: Alsalman, Yassin, 1982- author.
Identifiers: Canadiana (print) 20200284657 | Canadiana (ebook) 2020028469X
    ISBN 9781773632964 (softcover) | ISBN 9781773633411 (EPUB)
    ISBN 9781773633428 (Kindle)
Subjects: LCGFT: Poetry.
Classification: LCC PS8601.L73 T49 2020 | DDC C811/.6—dc23

Cover artwork by Saks Afridi
Cover type by Roï Saade
Cover design by We Are The Medium
Comic book art by Ashraf Ghori

10 9 8 7 6 5 4 3 2 1

To Sundus, Shams, and Yusra. To Falah,
Nahla, and Hala. My galaxies of love.
I do it all for (and from) you.

حياتنا بريسمتاء في لبتم أحمرم أيست بعتا الزمان

Contents

BISMILLAH ALRAHMAN ALRAHEEM

Introduction

I'M ALL OVER THE PLACE. I don't mean this in geographical terms only. I mean it, as Big Pun said, "physically, lyrically, hypothetically, realistically." Let me explain.

Growing up as a hyphenated Arab in North America and spending my formative years between two countries that serve as sterile, cultural "melting pots," I found myself often at a lack of words for explaining myself. My parents shipped us back and forth between Montreal from 1987–1996, Abu Dhabi from 1996–2000, then back to Montreal where I have remained from then until now. My high school years were spent in a segregated, private American school in the middle of a city that was shy of thirty years old. While the city was trying to figure out its place in the world, I was trying to figure out mine. We were growing up in a space where international students floated in a pool of apolitical uncertainty, while the nation itself was subsumed in relationships that further complicated the region. We students were never taught to process and express our thoughts. Living in that situation confused us and stunted our growth as thinkers. This is why I gravitated towards hip-hop and writing verses. We were young and ignorant. Not knowing the power we could possess or harness in writing, using racial slurs without knowing their meaning and origin, emulating gangster themes that we heard not realizing these are realities on the ground that youth our age were victim to. We were privileged in our ignorance. The space hip-hop afforded me allowed me to codify my hybrid culture and to process and express the incongruous reality of being an Iraqi expat walking in huge malls amidst American soldiers on break from war. It also allowed me to rid myself of that ignorance, learn the meaning of those racialized realities, gain knowledge of self and empathy for realities I seldom visit. There were so many times I wanted to lash out, and if it weren't for words, verses, bars, and hooks, I probably would have.

Text Messages

I carried the discomfort of displacement with me throughout my childhood. Upon returning to Canada at eighteen, I delved deeply into rap. I started using my free time at university to take over studio spaces to record, to master my craft, and to find out just what I wanted the world to know. About a year into my studies, 9/11 reverberated into all our North American lives. Watching buildings crumble as a reflection of a cultural and economic war was not an uncommon sight for my people. As Iraqis, we were used to sitting around a television, watching architecture be blown down by massive explosions. This was different. Masks came off and racists bared their true beliefs about Muslims and immigrants. Their radicalization rose to its peak, not just against me, but against the multitude of communities within the belief system of Islam—the diverse ethnicities of the East were then, as now, often misrepresented as a mythical monolith. A new wave of self-scrutiny and exterior investigation took over our daily lives. I spent the majority of my twenties defending myself, a religion, and a region I was grappling to come to terms with through lyrics and music. This experience echoed my high school days, when we were highly politicized and forced to be reactionary in our expression of culture and dystopia. Again, I found myself in a place where I was out of place. This demonization and fear still exist around us immigrants, and it seems like the web has been cast wider as the Internet has become a haven for trolls and racists. There were so many times, again, where I just wanted to lash out. If it weren't for words, verses, bars, and hooks, I probably would have.

I called myself the Narcicyst, a tongue-in-cheek moniker, as a reminder to never get lost in the self-aggrandizing nature of the arts industry and as a finger-pointing commentary on the increasingly narcissistic nature of society. As much as we are aware of the wasteful and destructive way of life we have built for ourselves now, back in the 00s, iPhones and smartphones were already a creeping reality. Due to my cultural mixture, I was forced to almost think ahead of our time. I always saw what was coming. The Iraqi in me—cynical, doom-prone, and conspiracy-driven—was very present in my work. The Canadian in me—privileged, moderate, removed—was also very present in my early solo work. I used to write everywhere I went—in books, on papers, on laptops, desktops. I had so many bars. As much as it was expressive, it barely touched the surface of something deeper that was brewing in me. I was too bogged down by reactionary spaces, preaching to a choir who felt the same gospel, and internally dismantling a barrage of misrepresentation that had been fed to me since the Raiders of the Lost Arc. I had no role models from our community. Even Iraqis in fiction—like Sayid Jarrah of Lost was played by Naveen Andrews who is actually of British and Indian descent. Come on, g! They just didn't know how to represent us anywhere! Saddam was our only reference point for people. Our generation was drafting a blueprint what would come now, creating a template for a generation to follow—the one that Edward Said galvanized in our minds. Our growing hip-hop, film, and arts community was in its infancy.

I was scrambling. It was very difficult to find clarity amidst the psychological warfare during the terror era. Ironically, the only place I could find solace was on airplanes. In those days, up until the moment we boarded airplanes people like me were under watch, under microscopic inspection and questioned because of our religion and culture. It was a relief to be afloat above seas and lands, not bound to borders or harassment from any form of policing. It removed me from the on-the-ground battles we were fighting and gave me a bird's-eye view of the world around me. In those moments, sometimes for hours and hours, I wrote some of the most vivid and introspective works I have written to date. I seldom shared them with the world, except sometimes at shows to gauge if people felt the same way, but rarely on record. This writing experience was personal to me, something I wanted to explore for myself. Rapping was like mining for the gold that was redefinition. That definition became a positive vision of self, untainted by politics and the ways of man—an understanding of the chaos.

I am an anxious flier. I am also a Gemini. I chalk the anxiety up to losing total control. I am not the pilot of the vehicle, nor can I see where I am going. It's nerve-racking, but in a way, it freed me up. Most of the writing in this book took place on planes over the course of the last decade. From comic books to short stories to poetry, these narratives and expressions were a therapy I used to cope with the low-level trauma I endured during the ten years of Rap Life I experienced as the Iraqi guy in the room. As much as I tried to tear down barriers, I sometimes built them in self-defense.

I recall running up from opening for Jedi Mind Tricks at Les Foufounes Électriques, a grungy venue in Montreal, to catch one of my rap idols, Raekwon the Chef. My friend Dutch was promoting the show and pulled me backstage. When Rae's team came down they asked for the greenroom to be cleared. Dutch told me to stay put. I was at the doorway of the stage and in comes in a stocky, blunt-smoking brother: hoodie on, looking down, reciting verses. It was Rae. He stood in front of me like a fighter, shadowboxing his verses to himself. He lifted his hoodie and looked me dead in the eye. "Peace Rae, I just want to thank you for. . ." You know, the regular fan talk started spewing out of my heart, as genuine as could be. Rae cut me off and said "Damn shorty, look at the wardrobe, B. Where you from?" I was wearing a military green Sergeant Pepper Lonely Narce Club Band jacket and a sidara, my grandfather's traditional Iraqi hat. I said something I say at least twice a week: "I'm from Iraq, but I grew up here." He looks at his brother and says "Damn, I knew you was one of those EyeRacki Afghani War N-Words (he said the actual word)." Damn. I had a real-life Wu-Tang interlude happen to me. But it was bittersweet. That statement was filled with love and rife with the ills that we hyphenated Muslim/Brown kids face. It was full of the direct American perspective of my culture—a monolith, a Pantone color. It was also a full cultural circle for me, one which hip-hop brought me back to over and over again. Hip-hop was the only place where all my crises met head on and resolved one another in my heart.

There is no vindication in one's search for identity. I have come to terms with the fact that I will always feel in flux. In fact, that is my identity. And as I travelled around the world with my music, from Dubai to Detroit, Toronto to Tripoli,

Introduction

Beirut to Berlin, I learned that this identity crisis rings true for many of the kids who grew up into the advent of the Internet and in between wars. So many of the same kids I went to high school with were dispersed to universities around the world. Some of the Arab kids I went to eighth grade with ended up enduring the 9/11 experience concurrently with their personal webs of stereotyping, shock, and eventual profiling in their diaspora. Little did I know, the same could be said for my Chinese and Korean friends, my Brazilian and Colombian comrades, African American and continental African classmates. So many of our colonial histories have resurfaced on the coast of the Internet's tide that we surf together. Just as the LGBTQIA communities' struggles have come to light and more clarity is being shed on the diversity, the individuality, and the intrapersonal suffering of marginalized people—we are finding spaces to have uncomfortable conversations about our relationship to both the white savior complexes and the hegemonic orders of European patriarchy on our genetic history. Feels like the time is now, more than ever.

I wrote most of this book on my phone. I hate my phone. It has become the extension of my skin that I never wanted. It gives me anxiety at times; at times it educates me; at times it has made me cry. At most times, it has made me witness to the most vivid of humanity's crimes, deaths, and accidents. Things I never wanted to see. Trauma I never asked for. I liken my iPhone to the Anti-Christ at times—I mean think about it. It has one eye, it lies to you when it tells you the truth, it can bring the moon down to Earth, and if you consider Steve Jobs as its father, it was even born in Syria! Talk about Prophecy at work. But I am also a paranoid Arab boy, so pardon my over-analyzing. It's something to think about though, isn't it? So, though the phone permitted me to write out these thoughts and feelings, it also is something I loathe at times. I need to find a balance with it, and this book is a way of unloading the download, unchaining my algorithm and reconfiguring my personal interface.

This is what Text Messages is to me. It is a diary, and it's something I hope you can see yourself in. I wrote it for you and me alike. It is of that infinite search for an identity. It is of flying high in the sky looking for a place to go and belong to. Watch out for turbulent times, stay calm, and land safely.

With peace,
Yassin

VERSES

False Start

False start
Beginnings always dictate endings
in the memory of the forgotten.
Like a book in need of mending.

False start

Young boys and girls trapped in Walmarts—
our consumer interim camps.
A family-friendly, discounted freedom.
You don't see what the Internet can't.

Not our land or home.
Not your mans or holmes.
Not your towers or domes.
Not your power or drones.

False start

Anxious Balloons

Between two eras—
errors and affirmations—
the Karma of America
meets effort.

Confused about where I stand,
I fall for myself every time.
Misjudgment of my own eyes.
I don't see them anymore.

It is quite clear that we were meant to be this way.
No structure, no sentence bleed, an endless day,
a sunrise forever.
A forever set in suns setting.
We mistook the moon,
sacrificed our star,
wasn't even that hard.

Not in the moment anymore,
we dwell in the past together in regret.
To a future filled with anxious balloons
floating.

It is very easy to lose touch when
you always have something else in your hands.
Bury the galaxy in your heart. I will follow you there.
This is love: a present together.

Self-Censored Phone Chip

Too selfish to believe I stand for the people.
Too concerned with getting balder than an American eagle.
I love me a nice textile, wool of the sheeple.
Pull on a reefer to refuel. Read bulletin previews.

So nice to Tweet you, he said. *Do you mind if I IG?*
Full of wit and deceit, too, warning signs of the evil.
You bleed through me like IVs, the nightmare of my dreams.
I can barely stare at you either, you always make me feel see-
    through,

like doubt to believers.
Filter my face to your taste.
You stare back at me with your one eye,
in pity, tracking my place.
the light of your dark in my mind
impossible not to hear you
erase
me.

Who knows what you know of my children,
my family, my thoughts, my preferences and self-references.
I will not allow myself to fear you.
Face.
Weak.

With you, I can reach everything and everyone except,
    myself.
iRonic. We.

@Khalidalba

Us

I.

I would rather like to ask you a few answers, or questions.
Do you ever put your phone down after a long day of it
staring at you and pick it right back up?

I mean, occasionally, while sipping on a single-origin coffee
in a cup as white as supremacy,
I catch a twelve-second video of a child suffering on my
      Twitter feed
and my soul shifts the Wi-Fi grid down to this one bar.

II.

Single-shot latte. Simulation theory singularity.
Gentrification cortex, Morph X from Winter Rage in GORE-
      TEX,
back to simpler days before forced debt.
Baghdad café. Folklore myths.
Four shores catch your body. For sure, flip.

I would rather like to ask a few answers, or questions.

Do you ever put yourself down after a long day
of staring at yourself
and have to pick yourself back up?

Rap Life

Sitting near the Telly, somewhere in L.A., San Diego bound.
I'm the man, the ego, brown sand Iago. Jaffar mango eating.
Greet my wife in Tango. Feel my life's entangled in headaches
    and righteous angles.
Now, merch game on upper deck. Pull your cards if you lust
    for respect.
Cut the cheque, and you'll get to slice a sample.

You want the cake and the plate. I want the recipe next to me.
Keep the taste in your face. You must not be getting me.
I'm Anthony Bourdain on game. Cook the *qozi* for you in no
    time today.
Blow time away. *Zaatar* smoke the Holiday Inn.
Conversating on what a modern day is
and the plot of they sin.

Close to showtime I never grow blind.
Realise the potential.
We are alive. That's essential.
Everything else don't recycle in death. That's sequential.
Disciple of stress with quests to be like Michael.
Anyone.

My crew be where you be in 2-D.
Split seven screens like heaven's dream,
while you loungin' in the mezzanine.

Presidential-suite dreams butter all for the doe, huh? No
    gutter.
Cut her piece of the pie. For lease in *Dubai*.
Recently high but frequency low—

Verses

Hyatt Regency flow.

My agency's cloaked in secrecy, holmes.
My head is blimpin'.
Lyrically, bread and biscuits read in symptoms.
Simpleton, know your limits.
Revisit mo' bars like Homer Simpson,
so what you think you're doper pimpin'?
My music'll pull you out your car like Grand Theft
Auto Clan desktop murderers, mad left.

Swing a right to Mashti Malone.
Bring me cups to the throne.
Digital life is easy to get but hard to leave.
Same conundrum:
verses with Liam Neeson punches.

Dear Father(s)

Today I saw a mother's wail swim through you,
and the sound got lost in your waves.
Yesterday I saw a boat sail to you,
and she was blocked on her way.
I asked you once why you were vexed,
as we polluted your will—crude earth blood,
and on a rude search, dug holes in you with machine bullets.
Or so the plug goes…
and when we felt the tide pull us,
they placed a wall in between us
so you couldn't stream fully between us.
Damned.

Do we not see what these oil spills are?
Earth is bleeding onto us.
See how one child cannot see over the hill, or climb in peace
because the peak is too close to the kill to speak love?
Democratic rights, or so to speak of…

Summits of my brothers in robes give me no hope.
My forefathers turned in their linen,
before we bore horror on our infant children.
In Gaza, the olive trees have begun talking,
so we now greet the rocks we throw, *Salam.*

Ultra-high-density sound bombs versus our songs.
We roll with a flotilla of words that cannot be stopped.
Our decibels level and knock on your blockade
as we scream *Palestine is real!*

Hang yourselves with your ties.

Mix a little bit of blood in our wine.
Products that we buy in lines
box us in your crime.
Dollars for time.

Cameras, I see you.
You've damaged my people.

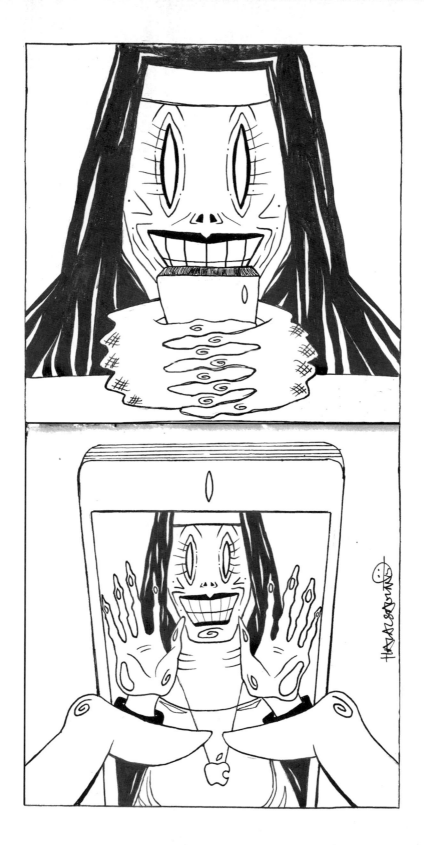

Baghdad: A Jewel the Thief Kept Trying to Steal—It Eventually Killed Him

To wake up with worry in your heart, I put that heart on your
    sleeve.
War is back in fashion, he said to me, I don't care what you
    believe.
Haven't seen brothers hoard bombs, they tend to let them
    shells go off.
Heaven is a million light years away, nothing closer than hell
    for all.
Peace be unto you my friend, the end is not nigh.
We have entered a new beginning, pay the price, you and I.
Prayer won't build force fields, but
it may build what remorse feels, but
it may not endorse your presidency for sale
or have man dem saying All Hail.

There's a war going on outside no man is safe from,
but man is destined to die.
Maybe it's time you said goodbye.
This way we have our friendship intact, this friendship of you
    and I.

Tourist

Who have I become?
Who of you will lose when I have won?
I feel the richest when I'm poor, but why am I numb?
I must be tourist on a star between the moon and the sun.

Who have we become?
How will I ever return to where I am from, when it is ruled by
    the gun?
Oh, my people, the people of the sun.
Oh, my people, the people of the sun.
Oh, my people, the people of the sun.

At the Club

The Digirati.
Blink and you might miss the party.
My vision Gaudi, living on a mission. Listen.
Human bodies go missing after precision bombing.
I feel the tissue rottin.' This is official war.
Ain't got a missile on me...
better enlist an army.
But you weren't ready for the fight.

Muhammad Ali New Era fitted,
Sib7a chain, blues bearer,
fitna game, mister vain
dollar chase but we split for change.
Everybody is a stranger... probably in our nature,
inkblot on the paper,
hit notches and faders, apostle creators.
But you weren't ready for the light.

Had faith but I lost it in Vegas.
Link blocks over think tanks in our radius.
Age of Aquarius.
Saviors of arrogance 'til we die in our chariots.

Iraq

Roots of my dates lost.
Calendar rot
in a battle of the angered, where a challenger fought.
Bye-bye fingerprint blues, when I'm thinking of you
we walk on *dijla*, then men speak of the truth.

Tanks for Elephants/Mechanical Surat Il-Fil.
Brown Birds hold burning rocks to your zeal.
Geometric star and crescent universal we seal.

Abeers's screams tore holes in the ozone.
Now her motherland knows no better than cold bones.
Brother of never me,
helicopter shredder, propeller hopper.
The grass is greener from the desert chopper.
The sand is whiter, hotter.
Metal shocker. Seventh chakra.

The walls of prisons bounce the echo
of concrete wails,

take out the bricks that
block the way to the awful meadow
where sheep stalk through unlawful arrows.

The land, broken, bleeds black gold—
half molds sold in bereavement for Iraq's soul.

So old we are, Naive I Eve,
skyscrapers and spy papers,
destruction of thy nature.

God's hand touched your shoulder when we were crying on it.
The clouds cried back onto Earth as we were dying on it.
Sinking ships don't talk to fish, they just dance with them.
They tell you the time is coming, and you just ask us when?
I watch movies that show me what to fear,
so when it frightens me in reality I know naught but to stare.
The world is yours. Make sure you do not share.
And they say all in love and war is fair. Where?

Thay3een, worldwide in question like my deen,
my being invested in triglyceride lies
reaching for the heavens trapped in five mezzanines.

The mysteries, the misery, the mission seen as visions
    beamed.
Light of my eye, where do I start my sonnet?
Finger in your ears beat to the heart of solace.
Just make sure you block it out with black marker on it.

So old we are, Naive I Eve,
skyscrapers and spy papers.
So old we are, Naive I Eve
skyscrapers and spy papers,
destruction of thy nature.

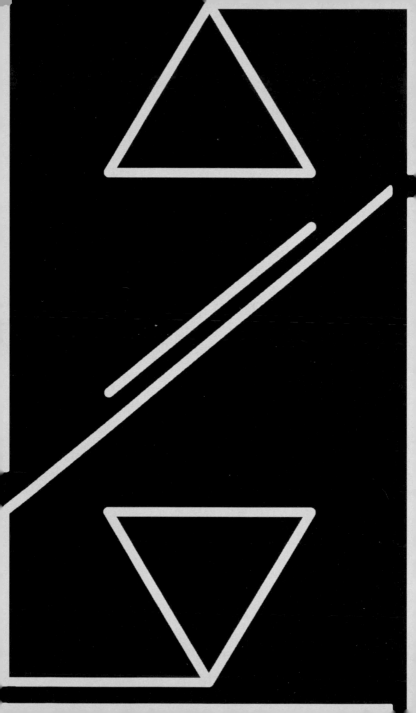

The Heist That Is

It's back to Bombs Over Baghdad.
No outcast here, all are welcome.
Doors open and closed policy.
Politics as usual. No Jay-Z either.
Ether me ya *Nas*. Drone sweet drone, walk me home.
No war except class. No class when there is war.
Students see the teacher die and become it.

A scene to digest, hard to stomach.
Tired of humanity. We have done this dance before.
My feet tired, b. Fire the man who hired thee.
Son of a bitch leaders,
your mothers would be ashamed of you.
Remember she is buried in the Earth you drop bombs on.
That's bombs on your moms.

Martin Scorchese couldn't imagine,
Couldn't fill enough bodies into this chasm,
Phantasm the beast, feeding inaction.
Thug Life never pays off. You're nobody 'til somebody kills
      you.
Kill somebody 'til you're nobody. Then somebody kills you.
This is just gangsta shit.

Numb to the watch but some bodies kill you.
You see numbers, I see children.
You see rubble where I saw buildings.
The murderers murder each other.
Makes you unsee the violence they uncovered.
History only repeats itself,
then deletes itself.

Field of Dreams/
Nightmare Meadows

It's my field of dreams.

Home run when I killed your team.
No guns but we build regimes.
Flow runs over filtered strings.

Desert Eagle for my people, I can feel my wings.
Stay fly, way high from the evil things.

Diamonds on your watch make your time heavy.
Climbing on the charts makes your heart stressy.
Messy old friends start confessing.
From the start you change, no end in the lessons.
Do you know what happens when a pauper kills the king?
If you build it proper, Papi, no popper stopper can stop
the cops from clocking, gun cockin', pop lockin'.

Revolving doors. . .

On the low, I'm too high for this.
No emotions asterix'd without the obelix.
Pyramids and obelisks.
Mausoleum of rap:
careers buried under fear of attack.
My beard furry and the year is the past.
Cold sun on hot steel, melted seal made of wax pact.
We are from the same source, fact.

Real—reverse the mirror and path.

Text Messages

Reminiscing on our kindred years
in the streets where the winter wears you thin.
Bittersweet like your children's tears.
Weird, I thought life would get easier.
It's subjective as the media's
perspective on graffiti.
Hieroglyphics was our medium,
so when we go to war, I hope you finally see me, huh?

I don't want to make history, it repeats itself.

- THE BIG HOMIES' BIG HOMIE

This Ain't a Movie, Dawg!

Generation fed on overkill.
The wonder kids, who appreciate but under live.
You know the drill. Streets paved with the oil spills,
fire ablaze on the soil,
shots grazed,
spot sprayed by our mortal ills.

Ew. . .
Moral filling in your morning cereal.
You'd rather scream when there's nobody's hearing you.
This is life as a music video,
except the camera is your brain and the actor
is your pain.
You hear laughter when it reigns;

it pours.
Love and fear, my brother, are very dear and live near each
       other.
What's a gun but insecurity and impurity revering each
       other?
And a tear when we meet each other.

Mr. Arab

There are several metaphors I could give you about the
    situation.
You don't wanna listen up.
Most Arabs are seen as bearded yet clean cut, rich and
    flagrant.
They don't wanna listen up.
I get it, I do. Some Arabic dudes are arrogant fools and
they don't wanna listen up.
I seen white men do the same thing to a non-light man. I
    mean,
you don't know. Wanna listen up?
I dream of a better day, wherever it may be, carryin' babies.
They were born to live it up,
never in fear of the life.
End it all like a movie, appearances typed.
Put them all up in a bunch.
Credits roll on a debit toll, so shredded, oh.
Mode on getting doe.
I just want me some bucks.

Since "Read" was said to the Prophet to the present greed in
    economics,

some are poor, some are rich, some blind.
Stress is there no matter which kind.
Investments are scarce, from the war-stricken to the tall-
    building mall children.
Wilderness.
Bald eagle to falcon on pilgrimage. We really need a Malcolm.
How come we couldn't lead without one? (Oh Yeah!)
They don't wanna listen up.

Text Messages

Oh man, Du Buy. Laddiddy dooda,
follow the Doe Blood, *la ti3bid* Buddha. . .
in '96 I was bumping Wu—out in Abu Dhabi

tahareeyat made me duck down like Dru-Ha.
Baby getting stuffed out on *Sukr*
while to the north babies getting
snuffed out for *Kufr*.

Bring a martyr back like Marty McFly proud he's with God.

What about Baghdad? Eyes bleeding, he said, Heathen, you
    speak of what God now?
You don't know what you are of.
I am lost in explaining what it is to be an Arab. We had love.
Aladdin and Apu or Adam and Madame Eve.
Imagine or fathom the Abrahamic steez.
I guess our history is just as much a mystery as yours and
    ours specifically.
Realistically, you should visit the East, before you even listen
    to me.

Agrabah

Time for us to help youths and elders the same.

Like hell to the flame, shelter from rain. . .

They watching me like I'm out of my mind,
cuz I wear bow ties and loafers,
but I'm really just one of a kind.

Benjamin Button frontin'. You ahead of your time?
Getting old as I grow younger. No hunger,
eating off the rich like Abu.
Monkey-faced, fez rockin' Arabs that rob you.
Agrabah, Disney cartoon from Babel,
get your whole crew bombed out like Kabul.

We didn't land on the rocks,
them rocks landed on Israeli soldiers.
The day that the war was over,
I was waving white flags in tan gloves.
I was handcuffed, jotting stanzas, tryna stand up.

The difference between the want and the need,
never the greed, Zig Zaggin' Zaha Hadid,
we, free-er than ever, habibti.
Threw a G on some leather and a three-piece.
Going to the East but I'm coming from the West like a zephyr.
Good effort. It would be your pleasure.

POLITICAL
ADVISORY
DISSENSION WITHIN

The Setup

Pinocchio's and Geppetto's love
pulls strings on your broken nose,
with metal lungs.

Visions of Malcolm X praying on heaven's rugs.
Flesh and metal guns, cheques, and leather gloves.
Lebanese cedar on the corniche. Let it run.
Never peace. Either we are all each dead and drugged
or somebody's watching on the clock when we're talking
while the feds trying to set us up?

I burn bushes and ash Confederate flags. Lettuce in bags,
you'll never have an etiquette as
human beings on their rebel for cash.
Forgetting they turned Kush into African settlement lands.

While the East is on fire, beasts are for hire.
The streets are on wireless and reaching all liars,
but we feel disconnected, scream: fall tyrant.

Free 2

Immigrant youth,
North American roots,
supernatural proof,
international truth,
superhero salute.
All of my people aloof.
What do you choose?
A bullet or noose?
Why do we live and pollute just to clean and remove?
Forgive me, I lose track.
Most of my people are under attack:
trying to breathe, smothered in gas
working a shift, pumping your gas
driving a cab, paying a tax, laying their country flat.
Open a laundromat, what's wrong with that?
Everything's relative, self in development.
He's steady been drawing the plan. Give him an inch
and he's taking the land.
Everyone's scared to be sticking the man.
It must be that taste of freedom.
What do you think it takes to beat him?
He's the cheater; there's no trust in that.
I don't even think my countries love me back.

MY
PROFESSOR
X
WAS
MINISTER
MALCOLM

WE ARE SO SELF CENSORED.™

Twenty-Eighteen
(Charles and Eddie)

Inhale a croissant while I stare at the wall.
Life's ugly with barely a flaw.
Might bug me. I'm checking the walls,
unplugging the phone. Closed curtains.
I may have lost my mind soul-searching.
What a circus. I'm wearing more masks than Andy Serkis.

Paranoid.

YOUR CHILDS' CHILD WILL PROBABLY LOVE A ROBOT

North American Blues

Who the hell's to blame?
Honestly who in hell are they
to tell us you can sell your brain?
Sasha Baron Cohen, Porsche-designer 911.
Smash a radio. Break a television on his head. Is
this another message or a song for our children?
Let me know so I can share it over Twitter.
How appealing.

Coca-Cola, bottled holy water. Soul-controller
sniffing coke up off a model's body.
Eat the food, Pavarotti.
Tastes good.
Instagram, paparazzi. Facebook.
Everyone is comatose.
Everything on overdose.

Purple drank mass appeal.
Down South, Middle East,
sad-faced happy meal.
Brown cow. Wildebeest.
Beef burger heaven.
Vegans always wanna ruin the party.
Everybody's Illuminati.
Play the music, move your body.

Mosque thug minarets. Lost love immigrants.
Be a master Ph.D, Michael Jackson B-A-D,
superhero-movie shit,
'til your people truly shift.

NO
THANK
YOU
FOR
YOUR
DISSERVICE

PLEASE DON'T FORGET TO BREATHE.

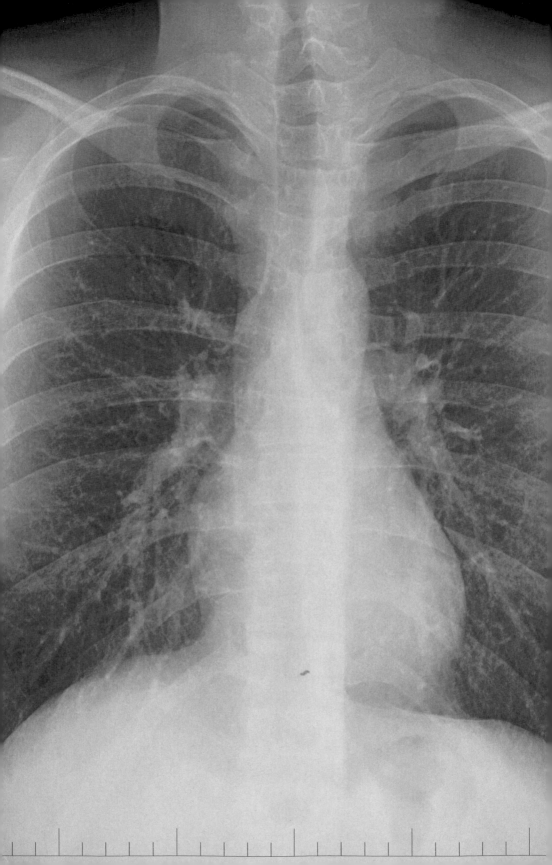

Overwhelmed

Our future washing ashore
I couldn't watch it. For sure
I saw an angel so pure.
She hit the spliff and record, of course.
She said: *Who said the pen is mightier?*
They lied to your face. The Devil brings worship at night to
　　your place.
I agreed and said,
We violent by taste. The food is the papes.
We worried about music, chase, influence, and race.
She gave me a vision in tune with a faith
before Muhammad dropped the Qur'anic mixtape exclusively
　　late.
Hit rewind. Lost my mind. Peace upon Him, the greatest.
That's why we never made lists. Take it how you want to take
　　it, ugn.
Instant Karma on plates,
paint you colours of a culture erased.

The medium's feedin' 'em laced
life. I wonder. What a waste.
Planet Earth, what a place.
Prosperity. Solidarity.
Murder was the case.
Raised, lost sanity.
How can we be replaced?
The vanity. The pace of life on mics.
They scanning me on tapes.
Rape, famine, no stamina.
Candid Camera your race.

Nightline w/ Peter Jennings

Are you ready for the next level?
The rhythm—the rebel—the devil.
Eye on the prize: the ring and the medal.
Sign of the times: Prince and a pedal.
Everything instant. Mints on the pillows.

Eat.

Bitter in the winter but
I'm better when I'm in the East.
Wind in the Willows.
We would never be
one without the heavy metal.

Who do we think we are?

Dead sheep in a meadow.
Only listen when the powers that be speak in an echo.
Only listen when the powers that be speak in an echo.

Double entendre—rubble over yonder.
Don't be surprised, just huddle on prompting.
So subtle our bombs. Lil' ol' kids just cuddle on moms.
Struggle long gone. Trouble going on.

If the sky is the limit,
then why am I in it?
See down to Earth when you flying to pivot.
Touch the ground we are dying to live in.

The meaning you lose.

Text Messages

If the sky is the limit, then why am I in it?
I turn flows to puddles on their bubble-gum songs.
You should be thanking me, nightly news.
Reach for the stars and someone dot-com them.

If the sky is the limit, then why I am in it?
Touch the ground we are dying on.
The news won't say something's wrong with the prompter.
You should be thanking us.
Nightly news couldn't anchor us.

THIS PART OF HISTORY WILL BE CANCELLED

Mission Impossible

One for the money, two for the soul,
three for the will. Body filled with holes.
Every high has a chill. Getting by on the lows,
we close to letting go. Let us die in the glow.
Don't want to own land. Let me buy into boats.
You eyeing the sky, I'm eyeing the coast, man.
Spies only drive in Renault.
I want that triple-beam cripple dream—associated,
    incorporated,
and a lie at most.
So what's the difference when you're flying coach?
But the business is really dying—it's supply and boast,
and your children have the eyes of ghosts that are hiding hope
from your order of operations in a divided home.

DEEP FAKE IT 'TIL YOU MAKE IT.

Thoughts and Prayers

Smoked Yansoon.
Might have to hang this mic up soon, like Umm Kulthum.
Trumpets blow for the pulpit's doom.
I need my flowers right now, all pulled in bloom.

It's just meme against the world, baby.
Looking at this bad news will make you stir-crazy.
Can't even gather up the worlds lately.
I mean. . .

Oh, yeah!
You got my thoughts and prayers.
Your Twitter-fingers too short to unbox your fears.
I do this for my culture here and my culture there.
So they know what it looks like when you're ultra-rare.

And the truth is clear.
Nobody really cares.
Is anybody there?
Fuck a dollar and a stream.
Understand what I'm saying? Yadamean?

Thoughts and prayers.
Is anybody even there?
The truth is clear! I feel like the end is near.
(Yadamean?)
Thoughts and prayers.
Does anybody even care?
Is anybody there? Yeah? Nah!

#JudgementDay

Verses

Got dragged on the net today.
Deep fake on the love conveyed.
These days you can't trust a face.

All your posts online, they got me judging things.
Offline, temptation for the lustin' beings.
Churches burn down. We combust with wings.
What does it mean to discuss these things?

I can see you envy our color.
You can have it if you change your AVI color
Whole world with their eyes on us.
Scroll down. Slow down. Don't die on us.
Feels like we are moving at a mile a minute.
Can't end another night without some violence in it.
Follow your heart, watch closer than the algorithm.
Can't be behind or fall out of rhythm

The Internet's advice:

Deep fake it 'til you make it.

I Got 5G on It

In these times,
togetherness in isolation.

A time to stop the clock,
take stock of real value markets,
count your blessings and not your dollars.
Listen to yourself for once,
they have spoken to us so much.

Everyone wants to go viral,
but no one wants the virus.
As she screams I'm the Osiris of this shit!
Ol' dirty people need washing more often,
cover your coughin' from the coffin.
Seems we are out of hand too often.

Distancing them from you.
Screen man needs cleansing.
These lands need mending.
Dreams can't be ending.

I pray for the you in us.
May we really stand together
by finally sitting down apart.
Slowing down came at us so fast,
being out of touch isn't so hard to grasp.

We are one, remember that.

Don't go outside.
Just as we have spread across the Earth,

we can be conquered from the inside.
The sun shines for you to long for it, for once.
These dark days I pray we don't regret
and regress.

Stay home youngin' if you want the world.
Closed borders or no order,
we fight the system 'til the fights in our system,
and we realize we aren't ever ready.

We watched our phones as they murdered,
only spoke because needed to know they heard us.
As they herd us,
the shepherd walked through the valley of death
with a can of Lysol and a virus on his breath.

We will make it through though, I know.
I got 5G on it.

Things We Took for Granted (0 A.C.)

Holding hands,
watching the children run in the park
and play in the dirt.
Until it became fun in the dark
and we worked.

Hugging each other after longing.
Staring at each other's hearts,
laying my lips on your cheeks,
and staring at yours when you speak.

Things we took for granted:
praying shoulder to shoulder
as the day would break and we slowly got older.
Ablution from
mad pollution, ad solutions, sad confusion, bad collusion.
Now we wash alone.

The sun for long.
The pinch of an insect.
Pass me the ball.
Swimming pool love.

Shaking hands.
Breaking bread in half.
Spraying it while saying it.
Connecting eyes with strangers on a packed bus.
Before we were half us.

Verses

Sharing microphones with peers.
Not counting the days but the years.
I spoke to my brother by text message
and what he had to say, stayed.
I am grateful for today.

Will we ever see concerts again?
Sing to me your lies so I can feel normal
again.

Don't forget your touch
as you distance from your wealth.
Don't forget your soul
as you distance from your self.

It's very early in the process
and we are never late to the party.

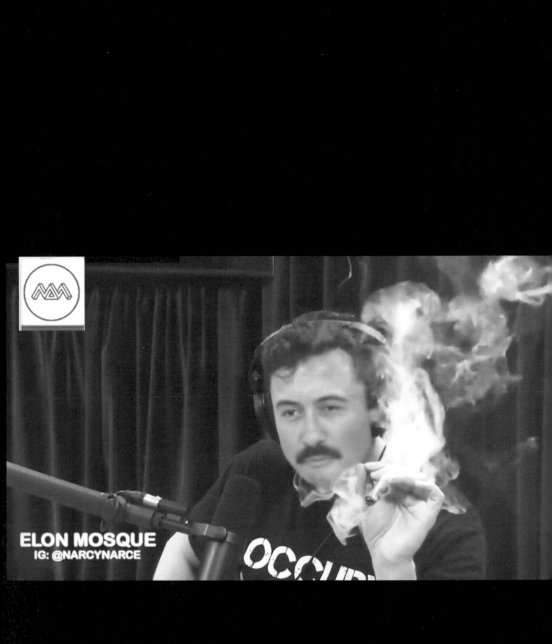

NARCE ZUKERBERG

FACEBOOK IS THE FEDS

I Know Nothing About You, Tell Me More, Dear Reader

write here please

Text Messages

On the Verge

We Are on the Verge

In the middle of the ocean,
hurricanes and trumpets.
It blew away the masters
sipping tea with their subjects.
Human kind by design,

what a natural disaster.
Asked the queen on my bill,
Could we end this any faster?

The Internet and their profits vs.
so-called ignorance of our prophets.
Live climate algorithm,
an Al Gore rhythm. Couldn't stop it (played out, I know).
No matter what you say,
couldn't top it with a toupee
big as a circle crop is.
Agent Orange is in office.

As Colin took a knee
men strapped our sons with explosives,
set our children afloat on the seas
towards the shore to be free.

How are we raising our children?
White sheets should never tell anyone how to be. Arab or
    American,
a woman should do as she pleases. Pass her the keys.
Skrrrrt, to the promised land my g's.

ALL MY HEROES ARE DEAD BRO.

At the end of days
I'll keep one eye open like the NSA.
What a way to go.
Adam and Eve on Apple Pay.

I Am on the Verge

People will love to hate.
Record executives told me to be safe.
Educational institutions try to put me in my place.
Corporations keep telling me I'm late.
Creepy, rich, white men in power keep getting caught on tape.
Too many officers kill Black men and beat the case.
Rappers and politicians keep lying and escape.
Fuck guns, what happened to throwing a pie in your face?

What is it about power: the high, or the chase?
Here's my DM:
All of these screens
have us distracted from our being
and the scene of the crime.
How many times can I stream so many people dying?
In Yemen, I'm trying hard, to keep my composure, but
        Myanmar... my God.

I'm watching Netflix and kill,
jets and weapons on some next shit.
I need a worldwide exit. No Brexit.
I've been here for each omen before text and the tech shift.
You know what I meme?

They DM'd back:
"This is the end
where have you been?"

Reply: On the Verge

You ain't never lied.
I haven't felt the same about America since
the terror instilled in little Arabic kids
by menaces like Erik Prince's brain rinse.
Bush, Cheney, Saddam, Rumsfeld, Obama.
Where is the truth? Why did you Megatron Osama?
While Trudeau nice socks it to 'em,
I wonder why a nation's interest is rarely genuine.
No innuendos when war is still on the menu
and the UN is filled with men
who pretend to mend new ends to be friends,
but really serve to end humans. Sheesh.

So much to say, but I am speechless.
Who in this room can we hire for a world impeachment?
A faith too high to reach it.
A spirit too stubborn to teach with.
For the love of our peace, kid.

We Are on The Verge

WORLD WAR FREE NOW!

IF YOU WANT IT

A Happy Medium from The Narcicyst

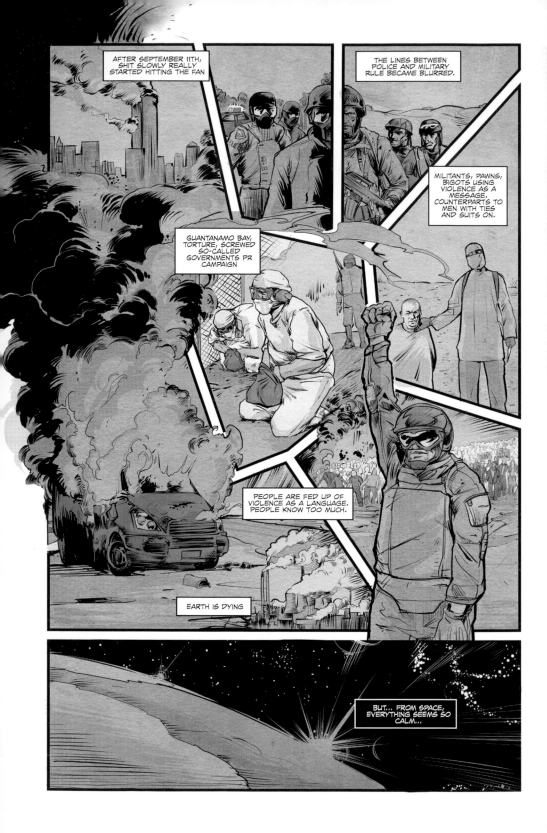

ART: SEDKI AL-IMAM

TO BE CONTINUED...

USER 1: Arabs hate each other but love a martyr.

USER 2: =(

Dear Jerusalem

One in the same.
Totally different.
Didn't want to admit it.
Needed someone to blame.
With the summers that came,
I would stare at your sun,
so we could be one and burn in the flame.

Love you though I never met you. I live for the day.
How could I ever forget you? I admit I am late.
Can't believe these men in vain, would even utter your name...
should be ashamed! I wonder what their mothers would say.

My apologies, yes, that was small of me. No,
I didn't hear you calling, regret has swallowed me whole.
I put my head to your feet, kiss the earth. We are blessed.
I put this on my government's name; you're flesh of our flesh.
You're a door to the heavens, from your floor to the seventh,
saw Muhammad—peace be upon Him—in his need to ascend.
You carried Mary in death, held her very last breath,
stood as Jesus healed people after he wept.
Oh, Jerusalem.

Even children can draw lines in the sand.
An office does not dictate a designation of land.
You paint a picture of a planet that is only a brand.
The devil's drummer's sheet music fits on one stand.
Singing off-tune with your soloist band,
Jerusalem, you belong to no man.

All We Need

Is silence intelligent sacrifice?
Are we scared of something we created?
The courts debate you. The sports distract you.
They always hate you to make sure they detract you
like love attracts you. Hate will make a man forget his
    namesake.
Political talk, confusion all a vacuum. Earth can be such a
    vain place.
Stare face-to-face with a tank, face case on case for a planned
    attack
and turn a man into future plan. Actually, everybody,
experience can turn a lost soul into a guided missile signed off
    on by an official.
The dervish lost his hold for a moment this week. Ramadan
    was shaken in its final days. They do say this is all a test.
I see people whipping foreigns, waves ripping the foreigners,
    babies living in horror, chains, spliffs, and Gomorrah.
Planes missing and more of the same prisons. All the citizens
    want is for the king to listen.

Picture of an Arab Man

His eyes saw love during war,
lived illuminated by worry on his brow.
Mention his voice and the world goes deaf.
Speak to him and hear pain in his happiness.
Flesh is a shell penetrable by shells.
Once opened, it never closes again.

Viewer, your eyes show, you are in love with war,
worried you might lose your freedom to him.
I speak to you and hear your happiness in his pain.
Flesh is a broken shell—
once closed you left him open to no interpretation.

Beautiful in his frame,
ready to change his father's ways.
His mother's lullabies echo in his darker days.
To the earth he shall return,
falling before your gaze.

He carried his guilt next to his shame—
threw it all into the ocean,
chose himself a new name,
found his range of emotion.

To whom it may concern.
To the earth he shall return,
a treasure amidst the sand.
Picture an Arab Man.

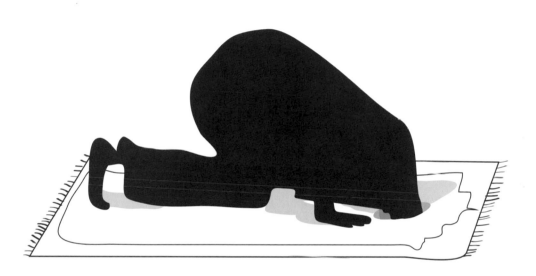

Khalid Albaih

Life Science

The miracle Iqra.
He and you are geometric—
the vision and the message.
The lesson is Mekkah-centric:
the teacher, the planet, the method, the apprentice.
Justice, peace, equality in a sentence.
History and prophecy, the 7afith in their piousness.
Dealing in my cypher I revolve around sciences.
It's time to reclaim our story,
bring our children back to the days of glory.
For her, for him, for us, for me and
you, from the source of our Niya.

WHAT IS LIFE WITHOUT *IF* IN IT?

Street Life

Street love, lamp posts for my pillar.
Religion can't cope. Dank smoke as a filler.
River dance hand dope to my mirror.
Brother on the block like a Lego figure.
Go figure.
American Bandstand hope killer.
She always keeps you up all night.
Nothing like a drill to a Sandman
so divine when he dreams of no time.

So said the greatest author,
people will be people, so don't bother.
The saga...
why did they not listen when He warned us?
My father
told me never speak unless they wronged us.
Awestruck

from the dust, we have risen mixed with water.
Reign of our weathermen.
Pain of our daughters.
Mothers that inherited the path straight to paradise—
under their feet from the street to the afterlife.

The Q

WELCOME TO THE Q, the club of your dreams. Chandelier heaven. The smoke pit of hell. On a lonely night, you would split your money with the flick of your wrist and bleed your contentment into the wine glasses at Gee's bar. There he is, skin light like the end of the tunnel, funneling your sorrow through verse and cleaning out the glass that will lead you from your first to your last sip of life.

How and what can I tempt you with?
At my bar, you can find it all.
The perfect message that I can end you with.
400 BC, wine of God.

Never a sucker for punchlines, he shot at you straight. Truth had no chaser at the Q. That's if you make it past the queue. The wait seems like an eternity, guest lists fall from the clouds on a Friday like this. Three nights ago, we were so lifted, when we left here the sun looked like it had risen in the West.

Izzy sat somber as a tomb, cold in his weeping to a band so sour, sipping on years of guilt and anguish. The hunger and pride in his eyes have been replaced by his detachment and lucid paralysis.

"What's the matter, Jack?" I said to him so rhetorically, knowing that this being our closing night and all, a sense of purposelessness had come over all the employees.

"A, I don't know. This trumpet has been my channel for so long. This venue has been my haven for what feels like forever. Since the day we met, we've spoken of today. It felt so far away. I just don't know... if... I'm... ready."

"You are resilient. We'll all still be around. This place is falling apart. We used to have distinguished guests. Rulers used to come here on diplomatic immunity and drink out the bar. Men from here to Koala Lamp Ur."

"It's Kuala Lumpur."

"Shit you know what I mean! I get everything right! Hehe. We will live here in spirit but we have to ascend, move up from here. There was a reason I brought you all together."

"Oh yeah, what's that reason? Gee has been behind this infernal bar for years, so aware of his sin of serving us this syrup he can no longer carry a conversation in front of it. You are always in your office; we hardly speak anymore. Addie can't even stand anymore bang a snare. He's too busy with the temptations across the street at Room Seventy-Two. His wife is always running in here talking about some snake. What the hell is that all about? We are losing it, A. Dee used to spit fire on the mic, now he's just singing and laughing high on that fire in his veins. Moose is so juiced up on his workout crusade, he doesn't realize his arms are bigger than his groove is. Let's not even talk about the bass and baritone section; those dudes just think they are prophets to music. I'm always on the blues. Things didn't shape out how we thought they would, Boss."

"You'll be alright, Izzy," Gee said in his reassuring way. There was something calming in the dark of his eyes.

A loud bang distracted me backstage. I looked into Izzys' eyes, and for the first time, they were stone black. Just a pupil, his iris hiding behind the mask of darkness and his apathy. What have I created? The End used to be the starting point of all local bands. Shit, they even made it to the cover of Time Magazine, before they first trekked on the National Geographic. They are one of a kind, like cherubs plucked from the depths of rapture. Their hearts beat for the glory. They filled our ears with a lush arcadia of jazz. At the peak of the night, they shone like galaxies in the abyss of a divine universe.

Stars of my empyrean galaxy.

The night went on as usual. Since last night, Addie has been sipping Apple Ice Wine from Eden. The messenger girls had been setting up the entire production, lining up everyone from the musicians to the cooks for my special announcement on this bitter Thursday. The sky was digesting all day, thunder bubbled in the gut of her rotten city. Prostitution has run with last-day thuggery for the last century. The world and this bar have become simply modern-day arcades.

Since day one, I felt like the underdog, pushing this vice lord and that police officer to do something about sisters on the block. Polly was a queen from Uptown that didn't know how to do good for herself. Always coming around looking depleted, eaten away at the core by the way men had mishandled her. "Dollar, dollar bill, y'all," she would scream down the block, soul colder than time. I've seen her go from a young lady to an old burden.

My 4:30 p.m. cigarette out the backdoor is a ritual. I long ago started to loathe seeing her like this. Addicted to the experience of peering out a gateway to the world outside my business, I developed guilt for the way my people came up in the cold streets of our motherland as though I were the reason for their suffering. By 4:37 p.m., I was back to being the overseer. Breathing back, nicotine tastes vivid when it's washed down with mutiny. My second break at seven was always the most fulfilling.

Walking down out of the doorframe to the backstage steps always reminded me of when Mo dropped his bass and it split right down the middle. "Two sides to every note," he said, "divide and conquer." I never knew how he learned to speak so eloquently. The brother couldn't read when I met him, but he understood more than most. And there he was again today, plucking away at the depth of his heart, reading notes out of thin air. Always see flat and be sharp, saviour days where the trees walk and the seas talk. "Mo, you ready?" I would ask him every night. "Ready as you are, Boss. I just read the notes. . ." he would always play back. Beautiful music it was indeed. Let's just say the hymns of their harmony set the tone for our entire lives. Our money revolved around it, our livelihood and sanctuary, our kinship, and our fears. I wonder where they will all be, tomorrow. The fears that is.

The Q

"IT WAS A SNAKE NOT A MAN!!!! YOU ARE SO WEAK!!!"

You heard Eva screaming every night. Every. Day. And. Night. I should have never introduced those two. Somewhere between the sex and the weed, the fruit of their love disintegrated into the ashes of the rest. Addie, of course, I should have spoken to when he first turned trick. But what are you to do of a lesser man? Let him be, he will learn on his own. Those juices never did satisfy him from the fertile crescents he polluted to the vines ripped out of earth to become his wine, her whine. Not that she wasn't running around swindling men into the fortress of her riches. In bed, that booty was priceless, pirated and sunken to the bottom of your searing lust. I could never really say anything to her. Addie always tried to cover her up as a silent yet loyal person. I knew she had a mind of her own. Even as a pawn, she moved as she pleased. The game they played was tired. Even more tired than I am.

So there I stood. And he fell kneeling into a porcelain tunnel to the sewers of his gut. He was like a receptacle for abuse. He took it so far, inanimate objects such as bottles and needles beat him 'til his soul would cry ethereal tears. Imagine that, glowing multi-dimensional fluid chunks of heavenly water. But I have never seen him like this. She ran out on him today. He pushed the wrong buttons and boom, everything has fallen apart. Holding his head up from swimming in his own pain I could feel the weight on his shoulders. Perfect for a drummer. "You should have shuffled to her beat, joe." He had no idea what song I was talking about. I drag him out the bathroom stall onto the backstage couch as he mumbles something about covering up his body parts with tree children. "Pictures, feed them piccccccccccctures!! That's what is missing, A! Pictures!" So I whipped out my phone and took a picture. "Picture this, tomorrow you have no excuse Addie, none. I immigrated here with NOTHING but a dream and a thought. You had everything at birth. . . wake the fuck up! You're slipping down that ladder. No wonder she calls you a snake." This was the first time I ever spoke to him this way. "You're jjjjjudging meeee?" he burped.

"After all I've done for you, me? Look at HER! This is all back-wards right now, can we talk about this later?" I walked out a hater, when I'd been trying to help. That's why I never got involved in the first place.

I walked out into the club. Izzy was asleep at the bar and Gee was gazing at him, eyes glassy as the cups he was washing. Mo was hanging with Alejandro and Huss, two of his best friends that always brought out the best in him. He'd grown up with them and knew of nothing but that past. He was still young, too, came in after Jess left the band. Abraham was steadily mopping away at the floors before open. "They are shiny enough, you can stop digging at the concrete Abe."

"King, these floors have seen everything. They have held everything. I clean these floors as though the blood of my son was spilt on them."

"Calm down. . ."

"No calming me! No longer will I scrub these floors for you or run these whores for you. You can keep this place as dirty as you want. But my name? I have a reputation to keep, I will sacrifice every ounce of my energy until this is over, and you will never speak to me again. Is that a deal?"

"That's a deal," I muttered to him. Just another one of his rants. Split personality was always his vice. Goddamn Geminis. We really are losing it. Whatever it is.

Front door panic. We are getting closer. Who's coming in tonight? Who are the constellations that will be visiting our universes? No choice for me to make unless there is someone. . . important. Moose was the most obvious victim of this whole tirade, seeing as he was the first one I met out of the bunch. He looked ready to guard the gates, the most poetic of body guards. His ten rules were so true that people wouldn't even argue to enter if they didn't fit the suit. "What Ap, ey? Hey, look at these fools trying to get in line at 6 p.m.," he chuckled at me. "We don't open for another six hours! You really are crazy for shutting this place down. . ." "Crazy as the gods were, they knew when the right day had come to lay their heads to rest. Having all these people's pleasures on my back has broken my spirit, Moose. Broken my spirit."

I started feeling old right there. It was nearing my next break, and I could hardly inhale from all the chaos running through my memory bank. Everyone always told me I seemed immortal, given all the fights I had with stars drunken on their egos and sunken in their ethos. I've had everything pulled on me—from a pistol to TNT. I was scared at times; people were out to get me. I was almost got, but there was no face to a name, I was known as so many things to the public, but never as A. Nobody knew who A was. Somedays I would be the chef. Sometimes a waiter to the masses. Once I even sang a song that put the crowd in a trance, spinning uncontrollably to my melody. Sorry, I had to boast (wouldn't you if you were me?). I forget the name of the song. That all leaves me now. I would have been immortal in another lifetime. Now, I was ready to see it all stop.

"The second cigarette. Maybe I should quit? Thunderstorm of the century they said on the box. "This is the Thunder storm of the Century." How would you know? Have you been around for a century? Did you see that last one? How do you know how big this one is compared to the last one? WHO CARES? There is NO comparing any thunderstorm, any planet, any anything. Everything is unique. That is the plan. Nothing is the same. Each one of your fingers discriminate on each other because they are different. Your hands don't speak to each other like they used to because they don't agree. Don't you see? The rumble of our planet is hunger—its hunger for cleanliness. She weeps on your streets to wash away your filth, scum, deceit, murder, envy, greed, lust, irks me so this weather. Fuck this cigarette."

My bitterness grew. Dee was ready, I could see it in his eyes. His translucent stare was so clear to me, I knew what he was thinking about immediately. I don't know where he came up with his words. When you spoke to him, he seemed like a displaced being, someone who was punished before his brother was regardless of who did the deed. "A, Check this out:

I have… visitors… visitors…
Stand tall like a minaret… minaret.
When she comes I will never win, never win.
My visitors, come, let 'em in, let 'em in.
My loneliness longs for your warm salute,
Say hello to the fireplace. Wood would scream if it could dream.
You catch my flow? Is that a good stream? Seems…
I have… visitors… visitors.

What you think?"

"I don't think, I know. Where was that from?"

"The first night. The opening night! I found it, it was in my brain! I found it!"

I smiled at him like he was a child. You know, the it's-gonna-be-OK smile. "I'll be in the office, Dce."

***

8:42 p.m.

Nothing's different, everything is the same. Everything is different, nothing's the same. I feel so clouded today. Sitting at my desk I get the urge to rip all these stubs to shreds or get my shotgun and shoot the shit out of this hunk of laminated wood. I could set fire to the entire club—do something really drastic, just to shock people. Just for once, I want people to know who I am. I want to come out on the news and tell the entire city that their misery has made me rich. In three hours and eight minutes, I will be officially retired. Enough. Do I regret anything? Some things yes, but in the grand scheme, naw… everything is written as we say. It was great while it lasted. Bring the curtains down before they come up tonight, clean the bearings so they don't make a sound. Tonight, I will host the show. In the history of our Friday to Sunday openings, I have never once hosted the show. Tonight I will be A. Out in the spotlight, sound man clear my mic for action. Ladies and gentlemen, get ready. We are taking over your mind-fuck!

My train of thought was stopped short by a power surge of a revelation from Mo.

"A! A! A! I SWEAR TO YOU THIS IS NOT A JOKE! JESS IS AT THE DOOR!! HE HEARD WE ARE CLOSING, AND HE WANTS TO PLAY WITH US TONIGHT! WHHHHHAAAA?!" he said running in and out my office door.

I am shocked. Jess had sworn off this place even though I left the door open to him forever. He knew he would have to get closure one of these days. When he left, I wasn't sure how he would ever come back the same. "Let him in. He is always welcome here." I stumbled back into my mind to see the whole family hugging and screaming in joy. "A, I killed the demons, A. I had to come back to tell you once and for all, I feel better now." I watched him wallow in his own happiness for once, allowing him to feel free in my home for good. I do not want any more animosity here. This is the final moment. "You know I always loved you like you were my son. Welcome back. Come to my office. Let's talk."

He told me why he had left. He told me that it had come time to seek out revenge on his father's murderer. He had been in hiding down south for the last decade, aware that he had been framed before he even committed a crime. He said, as he arrived at the meeting place of his showdown, he'd found his body with an eye gauged out. There was the murderer, pointing a rusty knife at Jess, ready to kill him on his way out. Jess had snuffed him and run. He ran from the police, from the high-command security forces. He run as far as he could.

He looks completely different than how we had imagined him to look. His tan is dark, his hair has become long and thick. "You look like a different man." I said to him; the statement was somewhere between a compliment and a "holy shit you look old." He took it well.

An hour left.

My anxiety was eating me alive. The band was setting up on the stage, everyone but Izzy. He was still at the bar, downing shots. "What's the matter? You are the backbone of this moment. Tonight is your night; shine, SHINE," I said to him projecting my stress into his aura like a bullet to the brain. "Moonshine. Fuckin' end of my duty, ey. So cold when I feel this way . . . blablafuckingblabla. Where's my trumpet?" He got off the stool. "Hold my brass, I gotta go spread my wings, if you know what I mean. . ." He handed me his prized trumpet. I bought him this voice when we first opened. He never changed it, shined it every night, played it better and better by the second. I've always tried to play instruments, but I don't have the lips for this one. Let alone the arms for a drum, or the hand-eye coordination to play a stringed instrument. Must feel good to be able to communicate to a crowd. I'm more of the overseer type. I've always felt emotionally mute. What is happening to me? I held back my tears as though they were rioters at a government office, but my barricade was being broken in, all the shields and defenses in the world weren't ready for my breakdown. I ran to the office placing Izzys' trumpet on the stage next to Mo's Bass. People trickled in. The End is beginning its final soundcheck. I freak the fuck out.

As I composed myself, I dropped all my emotions. 11:30 p.m. Half an hour 'til showtime. Everyone is in motion. All is in place. My beautiful, beautiful ugliness, you are my child. What was once the haven of my passion is now the coffin of my disarray. What is my purpose after this hell-bound train stops at its destination? When I lock the gate tonight, will they come knocking the next day? Will I open the door? Look at these people, spilling alcohol on each other, laughing like hyenas, drooling at their own animalistic behavior. Humans have always made me feel like I don't belong. Their dreams and aspirations are so one dimensional. If you step back, you'll be able to see the bigger picture. There is nothing behind me. I invite you to take a peek. Step back. Now, you see it? It is beyond your fondling, your belligerence, your piss on my toilet seats, your vomit on my floors, your semen on my walls, and your addictions at my bar. Check your jacket and soul at the door tonight, there will be no turning back. Seems like you people are happy to leave this all behind. I grew out of the clubbing phase early. That's why I could run this place so smoothly. We had our fair share of scares, but finances are just numbers crunching away at each other and multiplying. You can always find a way. I make my way around the tables and through the corridor towards the stage entrance, the ceiling and floor seem to be closing in on me and crushing me down. Or should I say up? As I step on stage, the shadows around the spotlight help me disappear. Fat chance I will ever be noticed. If I can't see them, they can't see me.

"Ladies and gentlemen, welcome to the closing of the Q," I said so slowly I could swear nobody understood me. As I sweat my clothes into disintegration, I looked over at Izzy. His eyes closed; he was entranced by the hi-hat, counting away to his moment of truth. 3-2-1, 3-2-1, 3-2-1, boom bap too da da, 3-2-1, 3-2-1, 3-2-1 boom bap too da da. Seven counts of that sequence and we are ready for the song of our lives.

"Today the End will be playing out a special rendition of "First Day." Our opening night is our closing night, friends and enemies. May the music cleanse your souls. I would like to thank you all for your support, love, and presence in our lives. I hope you lived vicariously through our tunes and parties. Without further ado, I present to you THE END."

We were on count five at this point. 3-2-1, 3-2-1, 3-2-1 boom bap too da. Izzy never looked so free in his life. I could see the lights bouncing off his frame, as though he were the light and his vessel were simply the shadow of time. On the final count, Izzy opened his eyes and stared right through me. With a smirk in his eyes, he inhales a breath deep enough to relieve all my anxiety and reluctance. This is what we were born for. We are the kings and queens of tomorrow. You are the ex-hailed. Welcome to our heaven's people. The landslide of your deeds. The judgement of your rhythm. His lips reach the spout of his trumpet and his eyes close again. He exhales into his trumpet.

Ancestor

As your body enters the earth to be buried, I unearth the
buried memories rising with you.

As my grandfather lay in his own dementia, he would repeat
a story to me. During his stint as Mayor of Basra, he
experienced many colonial remnants and visits from
diplomats checking the state of their long-lost colony,
or so to speak. A certain British man would visit several
times, and they would walk along the Shaat Al-'Arab
talking and updating each other.

He told me that he would tell the man of the fish in the water,
how they counter each other and don't face each other;
they almost battle each other for survival in a big struggle
for space.

The British man looked down upon the water, with a smile.
"That's how we like it to be Jamal. That's how we like it to
be."

And he would repeat the story from the beginning again. And
again. And again.

LOVE
YOU

EARTH
IS
BEATIFUL

WE
ARE
TREE!

CAN
WE,
PIAY?

BABA
CAN
YOU
PUT
YOUR
PHONE
DOWN

Baby Boy

I used to think I was grown up until I met you
and saw who I had really become. Time is like a shadow;
it is always with you, but there are days where you lose track
    of it.
It makes you forget who you were and what you want to be.

Baba, can you put your phone down?
Did you see the size of that bug? I love you.
Where are we going next?
THIS IS SO EXCITING.
That really hurts my feelings.
Can I play video games? Why not? When?
Baba, you're the best.
Why did you do that?
Can I come with you?

Actually, time is like stepping back from a painting,
as you get older, you seem to only think about the bigger
    picture
while trying to hold onto certain details—
usually the painful ones because they color you different. I'm
    sorry, Habibi.
It's beautiful don't you think? It's beautiful like how you
    think.

That's funny.
Sub7anAllah.
Baba, do you think we can go running today?
Baba, can you play my music folder?
Earth is really an amazing place.
I don't want to go to school.

127

Can I play Nintendo?
I love you.

Jiddu always used to say, I love you more.
You have no idea what I love you for.
I can't even put it in words.
I hope the world is good to you. Please eat,
brush your teeth, and wash your hands. It's time to sleep.

SUNDUS ABDUL HADI

I Love You

I used to love you, but now I realise I can't live without you. Is
    that a problem?
What if one of us is gone but we made these babies? Where do
    I go from there?

How do I know I did the right thing? Am I wrong for thinking
    this?
When life flashes in front of your eyes, do you realise that it's
    been staring you in the face the whole time?

What if this whole time was just a flash of life?
What if I love you forever but in a moment when you forget
    who I am?

I am afraid of losing you. I lost myself in you, so, am I afraid of
    losing myself?
These are the questions I ask myself while I watch you sleep.
I can't sleep like I used to. Is that a problem?

Hold on tight. I love you. Good night.

189 Place Du Soleil

Dear father, I'm a grown man
but will you join me in a soul dance?
I see no sun in the horizon
where the stars burn slow.
Before our hearts turn cold.

Dear mother, I'm my own He,
a different man from who you've known me to be.
I see no moon in the horizon
where the sky turns gold
and your eyes grow old.

Dear sister, watch your step.
Move your mind from the right to the left.
I see our rooms in the horizon
where the clouds grew whole
and a horn blew notes.

Dear lover, you might not find me
because we write love blindly.
I see no room in the horizon,
just a bed of roses,
a life that never closes.

Dearest son, you are the one.
The reflection I stared at for three decades now
that never aged.
No war I could wage would ever
justify my love for you.
I hope to never disappoint your heart or
have you carry the burdens of my father.

Dearest daughter, I will be your martyr.
Take me back to innocence,
show me a world before men, before me,
even before then.
Let me find my soul again with you.
I dream to ascend to the place you live in,
best friend.

Lovemakin'

hub oo iman would you be mine?
I can't front or ever put you behind.
Push you to rewind,
all for the play, fast forward your time
and pause just to pray.

The laws of the day end broken by night.
Nothing left to say when it's spoken by sight.
Light, or the touch of you, burns inside.
Lady take your turn and dive.

Crazy this world won't let you yearn and ride.
Stars explode when you sermon to me.
My. My, oh my. . .
die old by Narce, and grow young lying beside
a lion of pride.

Thirst in my eyes when I'm working her mind, searching her
	wise
river of the marshes had me surfing the tide. Glide.
I'm just looking for a heart with a beat to confide
in. Her heat widened, skin vibrant, we couldn't hide it.
Just feel it inside.

Between the years we had seen and the searing serene,
I was feeling low for her highness,
started vibin' but as shallow as I am
as a man I fell deep in the silence

swimming in the tears of her dreams.
Woman, don't fear what it seems.

Verses (cont'd)

Here's what I'm seein',
living in the years of Yassin,
no matter how caring I've been, all I hear is

I need it. Keep breathing. I think we both need something
to believe in. Fall hard whenever you change seasons.
Lay your legs all over the East. Let's get even.

Montreal

There is nothing but hope inside your light.
In the dark, I see you.
You made my future past, from past futures cast.

I wish you nothing but light in the dark.
I gave you my heart but never mind.
I lost my fire but you are the spark.
I was searching but I was found.
I was working for a sound.
I was running, but in circles, around.
I have things to work through for this crown.
I have grown bigger than the town.

We buried our friends here, fell in love here,
gave birth here, made worth here.
Walk Earth, talk, search for myrrh and sage,
her and age.

Baby you were meant to be something I found.
Lost in my own way.
I replay, forever, the day you are now.

Beautiful

Comic book on the bus, love.
Bruce Vain using change from his trust fund.
Vicki Vale, really pale, made her bust once.
Awful pretty out in Gotham City, plus one.
I left the chariot on fire from the rust son.
Skipped the chase so I could see how far the trust run.
Made my lungs rust from all the dust hung.
What a champion. This can't be it. Take your book of life
and stamp me in it.
Will you live in the moment? When it isn't as golden?
Will you visit me lonely, be my mistress and homie?
She said kiss and hold me. Can you listen and console me?
My submission is holy.
Cleopatra, I wanna see you after.
I'll never be an actor in the script of life if we see disaster.
We gotta let it go. Are you ready to grow?
I want to tell you, but you probably already know.

Word of mouth. I can see it in your eyes.
Live your life like everything's a surprise mirage.
Whatever will be. Que será.
Men are sentimental in disguise.
Never might have said it but I meant it.
Get it? Forget it.
Do you regret it? Who to credit? Who do I get to do the edits?
Your love is like a movie; it moves me with all the messages.
Foreign and independent, we touring with all the benefits.
Do you see me the same? Do I seem like I'm sane? Do you see
    what I'm saying?
Like the sea to the rain when we are feeding the flame.
Fleeing the fame. Ain't nothing changed. You can leave as free

as you came.

What a symphony, my glass half full and I'm sipping it

What is life without an "if" in it?

We gotta let it go. Are you ready to grow?

I want to tell you, but you probably already know.

Who Am I (What's My Name)?

Tupacanese,
Saddam Hussein philosophies,
and Mayan prophecies can't define how many times
we stop and freeze,
cop a plea.
Yemen on the mind.
Sold lemons to Beyoncé.
Air traffic from Bombay.
On my way back from Sean J,
tuned into shorty,
doing forty nights of yoga.
She had the authority.
Closed captioned composure.

When my mother called me with cancer,
I wished I hadn't answered. I wished I had the answers.
Selfish young man, life is a big karmic dancer
I'm part romancer, part part-time professor.
Heart, mind, and flesh, of a sunset
on you, in peace, my queen.
Sunrise in the East, I mean.

To the Moo'meneen,
Christian, Jewish, and Muslimeen.
Don't forget about the Deen, the *Sirat Al-Mustaqeem*...
WorldStar, Star Wars,
world scarred with Dark Force,
tweets from presidents.
Impeach the citizen,
this is DEFCON 3.

You got this one. The next is on me.

It Is What It Was

Save the party for later. These times are harder than labour.
We pushing part of the game up. It raises me Naughty by
    Nature.
Phasing like Narcy's verbatim arranges the same text.
I used to ball like Payton, now I save my pay cheques.

You know what time it is. . . Flavor Flav's neck.
To think this started with some loops and a tape deck.
From the cradle to the grave, the new savior of the day.
It isn't what you do, it's always what you'll say next.

Don't kid yourself. . . safe sex.
I'll prolly find myself some haters just to stay blessed.
We the illest in the city. You the realest? What a pity!
Really? But you're only trigger happy on a MIDI!!
Like Diddy,

I keep the J low.
And don't share taking O's to the head like a Halo.
I've had it, so if you see me fly, I'm hemi-high.
Lampin' cuz this game rubbed me the wrong way until my
    genie died
(no Aladdin).

Motivated

Motivated by these early flights to Abu Dhabi.
Muhammad Ali of the pollying in Telly lobbies.

The cerebellum Mesopotamian but Melli Mellin'—
before they motorcaded the Kaaba for what they sell in Saudi.

John Lennon. Middle Eastern Tupac.
I'm paranoid. All I really want is peace and pot.
Strong visions of the end on the beach. It's hot.
Sunset three times in the East and stopped.

If you know me? Fine. Pay me no mind.
What would HOVA do? Homie Duke,
if I did the same would you hold me to it?
See me in Florence where the trees be and my Taurus.
Rub a genie out the glass of Pellegrino in the morning.

Nothing

I need to be a provider. I need a stage and a rider.
Kiss my baby goodbye. It eats me alive every time.
I need a beat to confide in. Leave the demons to fight.
Move forward with life and leave my troubles behind.
I need to breathe in the fire, live within all the light,
and let it burn the desire, and give up on the fight.

It's like the dream of surviving is the only reason to die.

Nothing I do, nothing I need, nothing I want, and nothing to
    be.
Nothing to me, and nothing to you but we turn nothing to
    greed.

I want my people alive. I want a piece of the pie.
I want to read before write. I want to see for the blind.
I want to reach for the sky, without being so high.
Where our peace is alive, but then our people collide.
I feel the planets aligning or a channel divide us.
Programmed in our violence, because we fear our demise.

It's like the dream of surviving is the only reason to die.

YOU CAN OVERCOME ANYTHING YOU UNDERGO.™

Gone. Be There (Please)

What is written can be spit into light.
It's a given like deliverance.
My people are you listening?

(You must live your life.)

Your search for the right answers
might find you the wrong questions,
and a strong lesson like...

(you know it's inside).

Play your part. Never follow a script.
Dream huge. Be you, as small as it gets.
Know

(you know it's inside).

Speak truth before it would've been,
should now, could be...
all depends on what you put down

(in your book of rhymes).

You'll fall hard if you're climbing a ladder
drilling down in the ground to be God.
We are...

(crazy in our time).

I felt lost 'til the music found me.
Astounding how I didn't see the frauds around me.
Huh.

(Save me! They are blind!)

Sky is the limit when you're staring above you.
If you don't look around,
how will you know when they shove you?

(Say we are all right.)

We are all right though our living is subdued.
Earth, I am yours. I love you. Of course, baby.

(Lady you are mine!)

Engulfed

I am not in it for dissing and prowess.
Metal bird and Bedouins in a tower.
Earth fed on their cowardice.
Before the planet devours us...
look in the mirror in search of the hour of

self-fulfilled now.

No Time

Ebola cassette. This is that that.

We will get out.
The youth won't sit down.
Custom retrofit out.

Family structure.
Vanity culture.
I'm a fan of Rap City,
ultramagnetic,
kitty-kat pretty MIDI data.

Electro.

The youth gone.

With or without.

Throw back.

No sciatica.

Clips inserted.
Lips inverted.

Buena vista with a fist up.
Touch souls while they frisk us.

Make that change like laundromats.
Beat biff to the almanac.
Fit from heaven, all Iraq.
A pick-me-up for you to fall for that.

I WOULD TELL YOU BUT I CAN'T.

No Thug Life

We Are the Native Sons and Daughters.
We Are the Brave and Hunted.
We Are the Same.
We Are Amazing.
We Are the Hated. We Are the Favorite.
We Are the Change.
We Are the Sacred. We are the Strange.
We came on a Boat or a Plane. Both harbored some pain.
We Are the Masters. We Are the Slaves.
We Are Those Cast Out in the Rain.
We Are the Sheltered. We Are the Helpless. We Are the Vain.
We Are the Selfless. We Are the Blame.
We Are the Shooter, the Victim, the Home, the Drone. We Are
    the Here.
We Are the Fear. We're the Reflection in the Mirror.
We Are the People. We Are the Equal. We Are the Past, and
    We Are the Sequel.
We Are the Never. We're the Forever.
We live in hell, or we live in heaven.
Honestly, can't even tell you the difference. We Are the Cause.
    We Are the Effect.
We Are the Blessed. I believe that we could be the Best.

MY EYES BURN
FROM THE VISION.

HASHIM:

A Life Unfinished

Chapter One

"There is so much pain in this life."

To comfort herself, Farah whispered this as the contractions got closer. A few hours earlier, her water broke the dam of her womb as her seed made ready to sprout from its earth. The vision in her eyes tore holes through her mind. Her pain screeched a near deafening tinnitus in her ears. Her world was about to change.

"Woman, what is this water? You have made the Euphrates jealous of your 'river of life'," chuckled Karam in his anxiety. His dad jokes made everything awkward.

They had been married for fifteen years, and their first attempts at a having child left Farah next to a toilet, bleeding. After her third miscarriage, they became apathetic towards procreation. She blamed it on his passive-aggressive love for nothing. He blamed himself, naturally.

"Yallah, let's go. It is time, hubi."

He was lighthearted. She was heavy-minded. Opposites attract.

Farah stared through him with a vengeance she swore would revisit him one day. She carried vengeance against him for the pain of this pregnancy, for the nine months that he didn't have to bear a child, for his constant need to make heavy moments light. But she loved him so much it made all the hurt worthwhile. Everything was split at this moment. Her time had come to release the physical weight of her child. She knew that their connection was no longer natal and internal but a spiritual fate. Big Changes.

Her toes felt like chemically engineered dates from Saudi Arabia, but almost fake to the touch. Her stomach had taken the shape of a Monsanto watermelon. Her hands felt like cymbals smacking everything in their path with a crash, a heavy symphony with a weightless concerto. She sensed everything but nothing at once. The nausea, the sweating, the heaving, the cottonmouth that Iraq's marsh waters couldn't quench. God is everything, I am nothing. God is everything, I am nothing. She chanted this to an impregnable silence, then the pain rushed back and she wailed like Umm Kulthum's greatest hits blasting through the streets of Cairo. Time is relative, and it makes everything a stranger.

* * *

The baby sat eloquently between her belly button and hip bones, bouncing like a palm tree in the wind. He couldn't wait to see what was next. God is everything, you will be something, he was told this by his mother while he slept in her for the duration. I will be something, whatever that means.

* * *

"KARAM DRIVE FASTER, GODDAMN YOU!!!" Farah screamed as Karam whizzed by streetlights like a Ba'thi escaping his leader's wrath.

"You know there are rules. What if a policeman stops me now? What am I going to tell him? Yaba, my wife is pregnant can't you see her? Lek Gawad, let me go to the hospital! I am not a president... yet. God, I hope they didn't hear me."

"I HAVE NO TIME FOR POLITICS," she heaved. "YAL-LAH! DRIVE!!"

"3ala Rasee, ya gmar."

Karam stepped on the gas pedal as the baby gave Farah a punch to match his urgency. Baghdad was silent. He stared out his dirty windshield and saw no one. For the first time in history, he felt, Baghdad was asleep. Having served his years in the military during the dubious Iran-Iraq war, Karam lost two fingers on each hand and was deemed "unacceptable" for further military enrolment. Ironically, his official documents said he "couldn't handle" the work.

He remembers it like it was yesterday. As he was running away from five Iranian soldiers, Karam had tripped on a rock and fallen flat on his face (where he claims he met the chemicals that eventually left him "infertile" for years). The Iranians chopped off his index fingers and one thumb, taunting him with "this is for every bullet you fired at our women and children you filthy Arab." In agony, he raised his bloody hand to protest and spewed blood onto his fatigues from the gaping space his left thumb used to call home. They cut off his third left finger and told him to go fuck himself with it, before feeding it to the rabid dogs that patrolled the ill-drawn border between Basra and Khorramshahr. War is War. There are no rules. You know that, right? All he remembers is waking up in an infantry medical ward next to two Iraqi brothers, one without his arms and the other without his soul. He whispered to himself Al-Hamdulillah. His elation on the day of his suspension could only have been eclipsed by the moment he first laid eyes on Farah. He knew she would be the mother of his children.

* * *

It was January 16, 1991, and news that the Americans were ready to enter Iraq had rendered the streets of Baghdad desolate. Even the wind hid from Al-Rasheed street and the blinking streetlights. Karam flew past signals and road signs to Babel hospital and stopped his car at the emergency entrance. Abu Abbas, a close friend and distant relative of Karam, opened the gate and told him that the facilities were preparing space for the injured post-bombardment in Saddam's Mother of All Battles. Calculated destruction sleeps with collateral damage on a day like this, and spawns nothing but the ghost of life.

"This is the mother of all my battles, my wife, Farah. Farah, this is Abu Abbas. He sealed my fingers shut when the faucet of my heart would not stop bleeding. And he is Amu Qahtan's uncle's daughter's son. We are related you see. You will get to know each other better in the next couple of hours, I am sure."

While Farah was rushed into the maternity ward, Karam felt the uncontrollable urge to hug someone and cry like the two-year-old he was in his mind. Is he ready? Why this blessing now? When everyone around them has no idea if they will survive tonight, why does God give him this new seal on his love? What had he done to deserve such a miracle? There was no one to hug, so he embraced a cigarette and swallowed his tears. Little babies screamed as nurses rushed back and forth to their rhythm. The babies tried to catch the oxygen they needed. As Farah was rolled into her birth room, she saw stretched out on gurneys corpses covered in white sheets with massive blood-stains around their genital areas. There was always something so morbid about white to her. She knew, one day, she would be rolled in white, see the white light. It signified the end for her. And a new beginning, a rebirth. Abu Abbas could see it in her eyes, she feared the next couple of hours of her life.

"Do not be scared. These women came in too late. Their husbands are on duty. You are lucky Karam brought you in now. We will work together to save every last drop of you. You are going home with your baby. These ladies, Allah Yirhamhoom, were not ready. You, I can see by the light in your eyes, were born for this moment."

A sudden silence took over the room. They smiled at each other in the pure bliss of God's divinity. She calmed down. The baby pushed her walls. She cried. The baby cried. And time slowed, ticked away in uncertainty.

It was January 17, 1991, the day Baghdad saw its first in-frared portrait on our television screens without the magic of photoshop to alter the beautiful ugliness of war in all its dystro-phy and malignant magnificence. Karam chained-smoked cig-arettes outside the hospital building. There was an electricity in the air he felt shock his lungs every time he inhaled the sweet, burly smoke of his cancer sticks. Farah exhaled and screamed as he inhaled and receded into his own mind. There is an es-tranged separation between a husband and wife, a mother and father when a baby is about to enter our realm. Karam heard nighthawks squalling across Baghdad's barren skies flying in from the waters of his nightmares. This is not the right night, he thought to himself. An imperfect omen, a mysterious blessing. Al-Hamdulillah and Stakhfarallah at the same time.

At 2:10 a.m., Farah lost consciousness during her final contractions. Losing touch with this plane relieved her soul; it floated somewhere between her brain cells and the God's ether.

American planes pummeled the Iraqi-Saudi border, destroying the radar guarding Iraq's fear-stricken populace. There was a submerged world of treason about to be exposed to the planet, and Karam knew it was a product of years of repression. Just as his spirit had felt trapped, he knew freedom would be impossible for him and his children. His last cigarette spoke to him in smoke signals. Save your seeds, save your queen, save your kingdom, all in your heart. Farah woke up sporadically, her eyes portalled her in and out of vision. The doctor burst into tears, sensing that the problem in Baghdad was bigger than this woman's spasms. The earth gurgled. God wept. The devil slept. The angels were seared as hell froze over.

At 3 a.m., Baghdad was shoved into the oblivion of darkness. Shrapnel struck young women in their homes. Babies were disintegrated into ash. The air was thicker than most extremely religious figures' beards. The hospital shook as Farah gave her last push. The heartbeat of the Iraqi regime was unplugged from its pacemaker government. Karam held her hand, nicotine leaking thunderously as a tsunami from his pores drowned his clothing. The city lit up with firecracker bombs. As Christmas trees were being taken down in homes around the world, Jesus regurgitated his Coca-Cola in Santa Claus's New Year's resolution. Karam bellowed with Farah. Abu Abbas guided himself through the darkness with three candles and repetition's magic touch. One more push. One more bomb. One more life. One more chance. No more darkness. No more dreams. The baby squealed for oxygen. Air never felt so heavy. All he saw was blinding light.

An old star implodes.

Chapter Two

HASHIM WAS A SLENDER BOY. Growing up in Hay al Jihad in Baghdad, you had your fair share of sweating to do on a Saturday in June. He lay sleeping next to his younger brother humming to the sounds of the generators in the backyard. Electric Maqam. Somedays you'd get lucky and get four hours of electricity. That felt like a concert of lights, fire, and talking boxes. At fourteen, in 2003, Hashim had seen nothing but war. Growing up on war sirens, he developed a habit of humming every so often to remind himself that he was still alive. He had vivid flashbacks of when he was three, under his grandmother's bedsheets, eyes closed. The fear of that moment is only comparable to that of not suddenly not knowing who you are. Due to his much-needed reality checks, he was deemed autistic by Doctor Yunis Al-Sakhtachee, GP to a long line of politicians, lawyers, judges, and military marshals in the early 80s. But he paid no mind to the naysayers. Hashim knew that life was very colorful.

The television told him that today was the hottest day in the history of Iraq. He felt special to be a part of something so new. Catching that in the ten minutes of power in the house was fate in his eyes. Staying out or in made no difference really.

Sometimes, under these concrete walls it felt hotter than shrapnel burning your skin in a fresh sand dune power clash. He rolled his feet on a halved tire whose purpose, supposedly, was to hold off rounds of bullets that would spray the outer yard like an automatic sprinkler. He hadn't seen green leaves outside his home since he moved there with his brother and father in 2006. Mama had died earlier that year in a roadside bombing while visiting family in Mosul. His father became a ghost of himself, floating between cigarette breaks to the kitchen, hunchbacked as though a malignant growth made of separation anxiety and pain was lodged in his spine. Unable to process the grief, Hashim delved deeper into the abyss of his silence. Staring blindly in the direction of the newly parked tank, he saw the waves of heat mirage the occupation out of his neighborhood, his city, his country, his world.

"What if this day had happened on the first day of the war? Could I imagine Mama back? Can I?" he murmured to himself, loosely catching the post-traumatic-syndrome-ridden eyes of the twenty-something soldier, Joey Judasio, standing in patrol mode.

There is perfect chaos in corrupt order.

The newscasters called it:

"Hell in Baghdad"
"Satan Hussein"
"Hotter than a Harem"
"Heatwave Hajjis"

The news channels called it prophecy—a sign of the end of times, the beginning of the last level. It was a blistering sixty-five-degree celsius and so-called "insurgents" (read: foreign fighters) stopped activity and feared the sun, the dictator of light.

Deep in the 74th infantry, a young man by the name of Joey Judasio suffered heatstroke while standing in line at the porta-McDonald's in the middle of Kuwait's largest oil field/military base. "Big Macs, big boobs, and big guns; why would I ever want to leave? I'm in Baghdad, bitch," he thought. Soldiers left fifteen years after the initial date of entry (read: occupation); America's longest war and shortest victory. In reality, Hashim knew this had something to do with God. Deep down in his growing heart, there was a little flicker of knowledge. He didn't break a sweat. Nothing is different, everything is nothing, and different is the same.

Text Messages

The frantic pacing of the trooper had no bearing on Hashim's boredom. As the days passed, Iraq only got hotter, shattering all human activity. Staring at each other, lethargically believing that the other didn't exist, Hashim and the unknown soldier remained visions to each other—friendship based on existence and suffering alone. As long as they were both there, they knew they were alive despite the sweltering madness. Both young men were doors to the different worlds; they dreamed to unshackle their intertwined histories.

The heat was demonic.

Two weeks passed—Hashim still sat on a near-melting tire, rewriting the future. And, Hashim's Soldier X stood by the tank, looking left and right, front and back. Hashim still has vivid flashbacks of what happens next. Even five years later, as life has changed, he still gets the same reflex response. That jolting pain in his right sinus, all the way out to his eyeball. He sat facing his own personal Judas on this Friday like any other. A car drove by him; he saw it get smaller and smaller and made it disappear by covering his left eye, then uncovering it and doing the same to the right. It can't be real, he thinks to his soul, I can make it go away. Soldier X became frantic and aimed his gun at the car. The car came to a stop equidistant from his right foot and the tank's hub. Sand billowed from under his feet into an explosion of heat, metal, and screams. Hashim remembers nothing but the spark.

When the metal hunk of a Subaru blew up in front of him, Hashim was thrown back into the yard across his home. Fire and rocks fell from the sky as the birds did during the Year of the Elephant. Prophets rolled in their graves, God cursed the heavens and human beings roasted like sinners' souls on Judgment Day. Screams soared across the air like sonic booms, shattering the tranquility of oxygen particles into fiery bellows of angst. Breaking glass rained onto earth, showering the ground with a crackling storm. Bullets travelled in slow motion, zipping across and into human flesh like viruses impregnating blood with the disease of violence. And time stood still, afraid of moving itself in Beelzebub's pandemonium.

As he got up from the blast, he noticed his arm completely burnt to a crisp. All he could think was "why is there no pain?" Carrying his arm like a broken wing, he looked up towards the soldier and found him lying on the floor. He ran as fast as he could towards him and past the spent car-bomb. Catching a glimpse of its insides, he saw a charred body on fire, teeth grinning as though finally content in its fulfillment of its damned vessel. Being a human made him sick. For once, he understood his father's horror at mankind. "This is what you'll get," he would always say. "We come from Allah and may we return to Allah. Nothing but carnage, revenge, and pain in this life. It was written."

Where was the pain? He still couldn't hear anything but the muffled sound of gunfire, screams, and fire crackle. Running as fast as he could towards his friend, he slowed down noticing the form of another soldier. Could that be him? Was he not hurt? Unable to see through the fog of dust clouds and smoke, he began pacing forward slowly and screaming "helb! helb!" He learned it from an old British crew of mop-top singers/fast-forward artists in a movie by the same name. His arm seized in pain and he began to see the colours of his agony: blue, purple, black, red, green. He fell to his knees, his arm throbbing to the beat of the rapture, clutched his razed arm closer to heart. This is the first time he'd screamed for his mother in years. He cried at the seared limb, grieving its demise.

"STAY THERE! STAND DOWN! STAND DOWN!" said the soldier. He still could not tell if it were his afternoon comrade running towards him with gunpoint up. He stood up to face him and reached for the ID in his pocket that his father had taught him to carry with him everywhere. He would even carry it into the bathroom, in case a checkpoint was to be made between the rooms in his house. Visiting Saddam is what they used to call it—taking a shit on the shame of our past. You never know, he thought to himself.

"GET YOUR HANDS IN THE AIR NOW.... NOW!"

He could hardly gather his deafened thoughts between the pain and thirst. Where was he? The sound of the bullet exiting the barrel could only be compared to the first sound he heard entering the world out of his mother's womb. Rebirth, he thought, rebirth. The slug hit the wall of the house to his left and ricocheted into his right eye socket. It couldn't be, he thought. Mama, here I come. It couldn't be him. Mama, it's getting cold, the winds are changing. It couldn't be the soldier. He knew him too well.

After the tirade of smoke and wailing, Hashim found himself captive among many other brothers from his block. Yassin, a fourteen-year-old Basrawi boy who was also in his backyard and ran towards the sounds of exploding metal. Little did he know that something close to fifty-two militant Saudi Arabians, Iranians, Egyptians and Iraqis were headed towards the same street after the explosion. They had been camping out in neighboring alleyways, waiting for the signal to blow the fuse. Some as young as twelve were rounded up as members of this unnamed clan of henchmen, bent on hell's gate and heaven's lust.

Hashim lay in the back of an ambulance, blood seeped into his sinuses and out of his mouth. He was clinging to life by the hands of God. Four months of comatose solitude, seven surgeries, and two months of translucent REM left him soul dead. He woke up as the barbiturates wore off and rays from a flashlight pierced his only ocular portal. The nurse smiled—or grimaced—Hashim couldn't tell through the fog of unfocused vision. He was alive.

Hashim found himself on a military hospital gurney, handcuffed and unable to move his face for the sharp pain in his right eye socket. He would spend the next six months, six days, and six hours of his life lying there as a still as a lifeless young boy. On the second day of his arrival, a well-groomed soldier with a Robert Redford in Sundance Kid thing going on approached him with a slow, patronizing waltz. He was the bearer of bad news. Hashim knew this because an Iraqi doctor approached his father in the same way at the hospital where his mother, Farah, perished, God rest their souls.

"Son," he sighed to Hashim.

"I am not your son. Anee moo ibnak," Hashim scorched in his mind but could not find the energy to say aloud. The pain in his ribs hardly allowed him to.

"I must tell you your father and your brother died. We found their bodies lying face down in the backyard of your home. Looks like those damned Jihadees you worked for feared your cooperation with us here and killed them so they couldn't tell us who you really were. I really don't understand how they can recruit such youngin's. A waste, if you ask me. I hope this shows you who is on your side, son. I am sorry for your loss, but that is what you get when you play with fire. Well, that's it."

Hashim convulsed in shock. Nurses scurried to his bedside and sedated him into a nightmare-state. The news rang in his head like a cell phone's radioactive rays, frying his memories.

The truth hidden, the general stood back and watched the tears roll out of Hashim's one eye as he vibrated in the limbo of shock. He stared up to the heavens, knowing he'd lied to protect the young man, still he was torn in his duty and military rank. The truth was, Hashim's father and brother had died running towards Hashim as he was thrown into the back of his ambulance-sized hearse. As they hurled themselves towards the vehicle, two contracted "security enforcers" unleashed a tirade of lead-tipped death into their vessels, leaving holes the size of a dollar in quarters. From the Islamic to the Democratic, evil clouds the wicked minds of the wretched. The children suffer. The general walked up to Hashim's gurney and placed his hand on his chest to check if his heart was still beating.

"Die son, that is the only way you will survive this in your heart. Die. There is no future for you or your wretched generation."

Pity is for the weak. The weak are lambs for the slaughter. The slaughter had just begun, and the brimstone is ready for cooking. Baghdad was now the Hades of the Middle East, and Hashim became its Zabaaniyah.

Chapter Three

Hashim grew to be spatially aware of his face. As the pain subsided, it began feeding off the hurt in his soul. He couldn't laugh, cry or think of moving his non-existent right eye. The nerves were shot. He occasionally wished the bullet had hit the centre of his head. This would be all over with. Released from the hospital room, he spent the next couple of years in prison with a cellmate named Ibrahim.

Ibrahim was a man, approaching his twenty-sixth year—ten years senior to Hashim, but a decade younger in his actions. He, a slender, light-skinned man, muscularly defined with all the glory of a Sumerian prince, roamed shirtless in his four-paneled, shackled palace. His physique replaced his lack of wit and intuition, making him a sight for Hashim's sore eye. Feeling lonely wasn't so hard around Ibrahim, he reminded him of a doppelgänger of his father and brother; he had the youth of his sibling and the size of his father's frame. Reigning over Hashim, he took the longer side of their concrete home. Ibrahim called the four walls in the shape of a funnel the unfertile crescent. Falsely imprisoned as "extremist Jihadist agitators," both faced spending their entire lives behind makeshift bars. Ibrahim had been trapped in the injustice of his sentence for six months when Hashim was flung into the hole. When Hashim arrived, Ibrahim he chuckled as he welcomed him.

"Haaaallllaaa, As-salamu Alaikum my little brother, make yourself at home! You want some chai? Hahahahahah."

His bellow of laughter echoed, and Hashim felt a lump at his throat. Ibrahim had crazy eyes—not the kind that you feel bad for but the ones you fear. Hashim's nose turned as red as the blood of a martyr, and the cold air of that Baghdad night weighed him down to his buckling knees. The floors soaked up his tears like the world drained his freedom. He had been terrified of being mistaken for a terrorist. He lay in the corner of the room and cried himself to sleep. Ibrahim smoked a cigarette and mumbled "great. . . a child. Just what I need. Another baby." Hashim was no longer a baby, but a man-child roaming in this unpromised land.

The political unrest had left Iraq wired and shut to the rest of the world. No law could save you from the American dream. Everything costs something. And as bomb sirens continued to sonically score his life, Hashim spent the nights staring into the next cell's window. Every so often he caught a glimpse of the moon. He would seldom get the sleep he needed, too entrenched in thoughts of the loss of his family members and questions about what had happened to their bodies. There was no contact with the outside world, and God knows no one could speak to the guards. At least he got that cool breeze at night. Sometimes, the urinal holes from three cells above would leak into the mud brick floors and the smell of the refuse burned his nostrils.

He felt a void of color for the first couple of months. The military officers barked at him like rabid pit bulls while they smacked his disfigured face. Agony. Throbbing through hall-ways of his mind, he would dream of his father pounding his head to minced meat with the head of another man and wake up with flashbacks of his last day on the streets of Baghdad. Half awake, staring at Ibrahim in the distance, he would imagine the young soldier who was his guest for the last month on his block. Drifting back from his quiescence, he would get up and run to-wards the injured soldier and flip him over to see himself with three eyes and a bullet in the heart. The pounding thump of his heartache would wake him to the sound of Ibrahim washing his mouth with the water bucket collecting drips from the drainage pipes above.

"Sabah Al-Khair Hashoom!" Ibrahim would say.

'Sabah Al-Khara!' he would maunder back without hesita-tion every morning, the shitty toothbrush touched to the reality of his damaged tongue. Ibrahim became a close friend and ally of Hashim over the months they spent together. Ironically, they both operated as older men in their interrupted youth. Ibrahim received the occasional delivery of homemade kletcha from his wife, Sundus, along with a barely legible note from his two children Sumer and Stabraq. Jealousy was completely washed out by Hashim's longing for a family, which he misplaced as rage and angst towards eating any of the food that came from the outside world. He was punishing himself, growing into a man with no dreams, but phantasms of irritated incubus.

* * *

IBRAHIM BECAME THE FRIEND HE LOVED TO HATE. Every day, he would smell his sour, anxious shit ferment in the toilet, tolerate his excruciating snoring patterns, handle his obsessive-compulsive cleanliness and his passionate sermons of God. Hashim developed a disdain for the Lord, feeling buried by his solemn existence as the "freak" in jail. The weekly outing to the yard left him more scarred than his countenance; people called him short-sight, stump-arm Hussein, cyclops. The guards treated him as half-a-man. He was eighteen now, lankier and hairy. His shoulders felt heavy. Being constantly under attack while growing up in prison, he never matured into a man. And his turn the-other-cheek roommate, Ibrahim, wouldn't stand up for him either.

As a converted Muslim, Ibrahim held more characteristics of Jesus than teachings from the Prophet Muhammad, peace be upon him. His devout worship drove Hashim up the wall. God does not allow these things to happen, he thought. There can't be a God. Hashim received brutal treatment daily; he faced the wrath of the American soldiers as they abused him on evenings behind the thick walls of the prison complex. Ibrahim heard every scream, every curse, every thrust. As Ibrahim developed a fear of his surroundings, Hashim became more bitter, more bewildered, more confused and paranoid. This paranoia bled into an uncontrollable apoplexy. Over the years he channeled his fury into physical strength. He did push-ups until his arms felt like bungee cords. As his face approached and left the dusty concrete, he would get flashes of light through his facial lump of an eye socket. Those flashes came to occur even as he stood straight in front of his captors, before they unlocked the doors and shackled his body all over again. Overhearing a conversation between two soldiers, Hashim knew this was his fate for the coming years of his life. Luckily, his English got stronger as his will got weaker.

"J, are you nuts? You've been bum rushing that boy for the last three months. Shouldn't you be scared of getting discharged?"

"Chill out, dawg. Besides, my DVD player stopped working a long time ago, Jenna Jameson just ain't doing it no more."

"He's not a 'lil boy anymore, sir. Hahaha, you have no soul. Poor dude should be called Ali Clusterfuck. Just hope your fam back home doesn't find..."

The guard took a knife the size of Rambo's out, put it to the other soldier's face, and stared him down as his sweat beads plummeted earth like a rain of B-52 bombs.

"My wife won't know SHIT unless you want to take his place, boy."

"Hehe, yes... sir... I was just, kidding. Sir." He gulped back.

The guard put his knife back in his waistband and stared off. Somehow, he knew the occupation of Iraq had become a huge mess. The walls of justice had been torn down. There were no more limits to what could happen in Babylon.

* * *

Hashim would wake up bewildered, dazed, lost, and uncertain if he were dead or alive. That's when he "found God." Ibrahim labeled his awakening as a return from the dark side. Somewhere between his disaffected divorce from humanity and his spiritual transcendence was a moment he could only describe to himself as light. Pure UV madness. A late night after weeks of isolation for his belligerence and "non-compliance to facts of arrest," he woke up in his hole, in his own feces, with no senses at all. As he heard the footsteps of his abductor approaching, he felt his joints grinding. His tendons released a toxin so powerful only his pain could rival the distinct taste in his mouth. His eyes rolled back into his skull, the stump of his tongue sunk back into his mouth and his ears were deafened by a piercing tone, 'til the maqam of blood juiced out of his eardrum. The exorcism of his painful paroxysm. Doctors later diagnosed him, once again, with mild autism with a case of epilepsy, but he knew this was way beyond a simple physical ailment. This was a blessing, a message of salvation, a sign to a sinner, a benediction of damnation. The things he saw. The orgasmic bombast of interstellar faith, an explosion of life. God spoke to him like never before. He was God in his own mind.

Following his episode, Hashim and Ibrahim became closer. Philosophical discussions about the Ba'th Party versus a bath Party, vodka versus Arrak, Saddam Hussein versus America, human sacrifice versus the military, and God versus man where aperitifs to their food for thought. Hashim was becoming a man. The days passed as they built on their commonalities and differences and created bridges that Halliburton couldn't touch. In Ibrahim, Hashim saw family. Rarely would he think about his father and brother anymore. The reason for his imprisonment was divinity: fate—Maktooba. It was written, scripted, filmed, and released to the public. A love like Rumi and Shams Tabrizi. Except the teacher never really knew the student, the pupil rarely spoke the truth. Hashim had recently realised the only woman he had ever touched was his mother, Allah yirham'ha. Ibrahim became his muse and his raison d'etre, the closest he's ever felt to love.

* * *

HE WAKES UP IN LUKEWARM SWEATS, somewhere between his nightmares and this nightmare. Screaming.

"Hashim, shbeek? Bad Dream?" said Sergeant George Bush Junior of the 33rd division, taping on the rusted bars painted in years of torture and pain. No relation to White House Bush. His parents just found it appropriate to be patriotic in a time of war. Appropriotic.

"Yes…bad dream…yil'3an abook labul," he whimpered back in disdain. Hashim is twenty-one. His English is fluent, with a tinge of an American accent. All that 50 Cent and Eminem playing while his head and body were being bashed in stayed with him. The dub-over kind of falsehood; where 'talk' becomes 'tak' and 'now' becomes 'nayow'.

As the guard walked past his cage, Ibrahim whispered through the dark moist air.

"Hashoom?"

"Huuuhn?"

"Have you ever heard the story about Al-Mutannabi street?"

"Which one?"

"The one about the man and his love. . ."

"No." Hashim exhaled, slowing his heart rate down back to normal.

"Want to hear it?"

"Sure. There's nothing else to do."

"It's called Dead Trees. Here it goes:

'The pages of my life no longer hold you together, my beloved notebook,' said Hamoodi, salesmen of the mind and beliefs. Mutannabi Street was the lover he never tended to when she was around; he lost all hope in her returning to him on this summer swelter of the Shaytan's doing (the devil's deeds). Nothing is what it seems anymore.

I've seen him straddle the sides of books in his lust for a literary climax on days like this, unable to satiate the fruits of his mind. Dreams lived through me so vivid he could swear he was Hamurabi at night, seeking refuge in Innana, rubbing his sore body till his muscles were as fluid as Qurna's soil. Mutanabi Street was his red-light district. Slowly eyeing the wisdom that was into the knowledge that be. So far to go, he thought to himself, so fast the past. Nothing remains under his gaze in these dark days, as the concrete carnage burns a hole in his soul. Blood splattered on the walls of his old city, paper soaked in the tears of divinity. It only rains in his brain. The sun scorches his skin like the eyes of the devil. Knowledge that was is today torn to shreds. Where the market was once a circle of thought what remains of it was nothing but a memory.

It was beautiful to see the sky so blue, until a brown hue sculpted its clouds, made it a heavenly desert engulfed by hellish flames. 'Burn Baghdad Burn,' he mumbled. His shortness of breath was accentuated by the soot and dust. Hamoodi had been diagnosed with lung cancer seven months ago. The doctor gave him a year to live. Hospitals remain bare from the days of sanctions, unable to cure even a common cold let alone soothe the despair of terminal illness. War was his theatre. I was his intermission.

And he holds me so close to his heart, as the last remaining member of his family, wheezing into the days that he wished he saw beyond him. I brought him such joy, he never would give me away to any other man, never allowed me to leave his sight. I sat by him as he got rid of words, phrases, paragraphs, and pages. Prose could not convey his love, so he rid himself of it all. Religion was no savior to him, a slave to his own changes, so he cherished every penny it brought him. Fiction was too far from his reality to even grasp, so he sold every lie back to the public. And I was left by his side, stroking his musings like no other could. He learned me inside and out over our ten years together; flipping over me and touching my corners with a passion that no lover could possess, no imagination could create. I was his forever. He spoke to me, studied my disposition, took me and never put me down, sweeping me off my abridged temperament. Our love a pious creation.

The day we met was written in the history books. Laying between God and science, I was a treasure to him, an escape from the harsh summers of solace and pain. As the growth in his lung burgeoned and fed on his life, Hamoodi had no idea that what was happening inside him mirrored the state of his nation. As Iraq was pillaged and mortared, I came to him a hypnotizing epic, an enchanting story, a myth for him to believe. Our saga lived long, our romance undying. On our way home, we stared back at each other though he could not see my eyes masked by my cover.

"You are a legend to me," he said so softly, "the Jezebel of my saga."

The day our home was shattered came as swiftly as our love. The morning blared light in his eyes and heat in his body. Although he had heard my fables, he made me repeat to him our historic connection. And each time, he would smack his knee in disbelief at how perfect everything fit together. This was also the day that Hamoodi coughed blood onto my face and wiped it so amorously he forgot that his insides were tearing him apart. He cared not for himself, torrid in his admiration for my eternal frenetic attention. Devout in his piety to evidence of history I will always be.

The burst from the bomb came unexpectedly. It seared my skin and threw me to the other side of the road. As pages flew around us, Hamoodi awoke dizzy and disoriented, looking for me without checking if he himself was hurt. Finding me, he looked around and saw what was left of his workplace and haven of knowledge. Crisp bodies lay immobile in their dying, souls fueled the fires of burning Qur'ans, biographies deleted by the hands of his own brothers and sisters. This war brought nothing but despair and violence.

'The pages of my life no longer hold you together my love,' said Hamoodi, salesman of your mind and beliefs. Mutanabbi street was the lover he never tended to when she was around and lost all hope in her returning to him on this summer swelter of the Shaytan's doing. Nothing was ever as it seemed.

He walked the street, back and forth, daily, clutching me and shaking his head in disbelief for months on end. Mother nature had finally turned her back on father politics. He cheated her out of their pact and bond, and Hamoodi finally realized he didn't believe in anything anymore. He slowly retreated from our relationship, and finally, from himself. I watched him pace around his home in Hay Jihad, looking, in his madness, for peace. He could not accept that he was dying, leaving all that he had learned behind him. Why?, he thought to himself. He cursed himself for his lack of faith, he cursed God for the lack of presence and the invisibility that was the divine grip on all that was written in its glory and suffering. In his last days, he did not move from his bed. He wheezed his discontent into the air, the sheath of his soul fell to the pits of damnation. 'I don't want to die' were the only words muttered; he ignored me completely, leaving me to be an empty widow, a lore untold, a fabrication, the lie of our century. The cancer alone was not killing him. The loss of Mutannabi Street, his sarcophagus, the final blow to his shattered body, was.

Hamoodi died as I gazed at his spirit floating around the room; the greenish hue of his animus protruded from every orifice in his body. I wondered who would find this lonely man and imagined watching him decompose into nothingness. He left me a relic. Without you Hamoodi, I am but a poorly written present, an undiscovered goldmine, an untouched artifact, a wounded past, and a distant future.

Nothing is what it seems and will ever be same. No one will ever know me, or read me the same again. I have been deleted from your mind. And your mind has deleted me from our kind. I am all but a closed history. I am your book. I was."

Chapter Four

THE YARD IN CAMP BUCCA wasn't especially different from Abu Ghraib. Having seen both, Ibrahim and Hashim seemed healthier and more vibrant in their new environment. After the scandal plagued Baghdad Central Prison, they were moved here at the end of 2007 and split into different cells. Hashim longed for their meetings outdoors, where they would share letters or sit around talking about the mundanity of being boxed in or the "good old days." While other inmates kicked around footballs like their freedom depended on it, they would walk the square yard to raise their heart rates and push their spirits out of degradation and solitude. Hashim kept to himself when Ibrahim's family visited. He made no genuine effort to make friends with (possible) criminals and murderers. Everyone had issues in here, and Hashim was far from exempt of the complexities of being alone. He still hummed to himself. Inmates came and went while staring him down. Some of the bully-minded foes from his last incarceration home followed them to their new abode. The taunts and heckling never stopped and slowly peeled the layers of manhood left in him. The rape ceased when they moved out but the belittling jeers didn't. Neither did the fear, reproach, shattered sexuality, or disastrous solace. From the turnkey to the prisoners, everyone had had their field trip with Hashim's broken ego. And his ego had its battle with his mind daily. The soccer games would almost naturally turn into fights. With all the testosterone bouncing off the concrete, there were bound to be hairy moments that turned into machismo grande. Iraqi prisons were like Greek colosseum exhibits, with machine guns instead of swords and Americans as lords and Iraqi men as rabid dogs.

Hashim watched the matches jealously, knowing he could never be equal to those men. With no father and no prospect of someone waiting for him on the other side, he felt deserted. The sunlight would zone him out of self-loathing into trances of bewilderment. He would enter into transfixed states of abstraction, envisioning being with Ibrahim then whispering Stakhfarallah, Stakhfarallah, Stakhfarallah 'til the words started feeling only like sounds. stakh-far-allah. Stuck Far, Allah. This is not who you are. His rapture from his own desires became complete catatonia, he was so separate from himself, he was almost acting out an unwritten script. No directors, no screenplay. No glamour and glitz when you're battered and split. "You have one eye," he told himself, "you will always see clearer than the rest." He spent the nights alone in his cell. The buzz of the outside world kept his mind company between the frenetic screams of next-door neighbors and deafening silence. Frantic speechlessness—40-dB violence. The further he delved into Islam, the more distant he felt from pain. The further he travelled in silence, the more his mind expanded. He began memorizing hadiths and dropping them in his conversations with Ibrahim at the drop of a dinar. His reservations and actions became daily routines, teaching himself the way of the Prophet. His tête-à-tête imagined conversations with the messengers of God become more frequent in his dreams. His waking life was spent fantasizing about meeting God and what he would tell Him. Ibrahim noticed these changes in Hashim and kept his distance but never was too shy to pierce Hashim's visions of the afterlife. "The space between life and God," Hashim would state with the urgency of the truth, "is as small you make it brother. If so, why not be able to talk to Him?" "How do you know it's a him?" "How do you know he is not?"

"Ah! You're a smart one, ya klawchi. You're still a child, you will realise God is greater than your conversation when you have children." "If I never have, why would I want children?" "What do you mean want? It is your duty if you believe in God!! You discovered religion a couple of years ago. And your religion came to you over a thousand years ago. Catch up." "Children will see nothing but war from now on. They will see pain, pestilence, ignorance, rancid emotion, cancerous humanity. There is nothing left for children..."

Ibrahim sat silent, soaking in the wound of Hashim's life. He didn't say anything because he knew what he had seen with his own eyes was enough proof to make you believe this life is a curse. He looked back at all Hashim had told him of his existence. His skin still shrieked at the thought of the last four years behind bars. He now understood Hashim for the first time and was overwhelmed with fear and love. "You are right," he said to Hashim without a doubt, "even though you are a child."

* * *

On January 17th, 2007, on Hashim's sixteenth birthday, the court process into his detention came into fruition. The judge deemed Hashim a minor and unaware of the consequences of perjury. When asked where his family was, Hashim said with God. When asked where he was on the day of the incident, he says in the thoughts of God. When asked if he thinks he will ever be free, he said God willing. The process was beneath him. He left it to his mousy Iraqi lawyer to get the American oil money soaking his hands with the fuel of the overlords. He was beyond this plain, he was a free man and believed he would be the ruler of all things to come. The judge viewed Hashim's incoherence as ruffian behavior and sentenced him to two more years for "corrupting court documents and detriment of the truth clause no. 149 of the American/Iraqi drafted POW treaty of 2005." Some bullshit that was.

By March, Hashim was back in his routine. No brightly lit bathroom-converted courtrooms. No more banishment to oblivion. He had a date of release in mind; it was a countdown. He followed a regimen of prayer, and ignored belligerence from other cellmates. One in particular, Jameel, would spray Hashim with searing deprecation. He called Hashim ugly, small, unpleasant, child, retard; he levied malicious, heartfelt hate-challenges. Hashim would telepathically send Jameel message that his mental inbox rejected: "I am your God." "You will see my light." On the surface, Hashim did not concede or crack under the pressures of prejudice. He sat quietly as Jameel's spit bounced off his face like the sunrays on Iraq's afternoons.

Ibrahim was acquitted of all charges and given a pardon for good behavior, and, through his old friends who were now heavy political rollers, he steam-ironed his way out of a file and back into the explosive reality that was Baghhad. "When you leave," he said to Hashim "call me here. I will meet you and you'll stay with us until you get back on your feet. We are your family." God is Great, I am Greater, Hashim thought to himself. Other days, he realised he wasn't shit and wanted nothing more than he wanted death. His ups and downs seesawed him. Hashim became a recluse in his first six months without Ibrahim. He knew not what life would be after these walls. But knew Ibrahim would always be there for him. He took showers on Tuesdays, Thursdays, Fridays, and Sundays. Between woo'dhoo' and daily clean ups, Hashim had avoided showers and knew to stay away from that area at certain hours. His small yet developed frame made him fear the approach of any nude man that he didn't welcome. But this Wednesday was special. It rained on the prison camp for the first time in ages; Hashim spent it standing in heaven's tears. He felt each drop hit his face like a freezing fire. He cried for the years lost between himself and his father. He cleansed his soul of his brother's burdened body. He knelt down to his knees and touched the mud and kissed it knowing that his family had become of this earth. He was finally growing out of the cocoon of denial he had built himself. From the other side of the prison yard, Jameel saw this as another display of Hashim's stupidity. "God will not save him from this," he laughed as he kicked the football directly towards Hashim's rising head. As he freed Surat Ya'sin in the memory of his family, the ball jammed itself into his face, cementing the distinct reality that was his life. He had a life interrupted, there was not a single sacred moment in his day. Even God is not free of his humiliation. He fell face first into a puddle of mud and was covered from head to toe in his decomposed ancestry. He lay unconscious in the mud, head spinning like a pious dervish.

That night, as he turned on the faucet to shower for the first time on a Wednesday, Jameel walked in the shower and stared at Hashim with a predators' gaze. He saw him approach but said nothing. He kept his back to the shower and faced Jameel without staring him in the eye. Jameel stepped to the shower next to Hashim in uncomfortable silence and began lathering the soap bar in his hand. The kenetics of their energy cleansed the years of retributive justice between them. Hashim closed his eye under the mist of the showers and thanked God. Jameel reached for Hashim's body as he opened his eye back to the world. He dropped his soap bar and slipped out of Jameel's calloused hands reaching towards the exit of the bathroom. His heart racing in front of his body, Jameel let out a snarl and ricocheted towards him in despoiled lust. He slipped on the soap bar and smacked his face into the shower knob on Hashim's side, bursting his left temple open into a fountain of wine-colored waters. He lay there, naked, bleeding to death in seizure of his soul's release.

Hashim stareed down at him as the showers rained down on both of them. He had to do something. As he reached for Jameel's head to cover the wound, he heard a chatter approaching the shower complex. Realising how the scene might appear, Hashim apologized to a dead Jameel and left the scene. A storm brewed in Hashim's soul as word got around the prison that night that Jameel had died. He had been the star player in the field. A lot of people revered him as a leader of sorts, the first of many Iraqi men that had become reduced to football heroes in the fields of American Dreams. No Kevin Costner could build shit for these men. Another father figure in the dirt. Hashim stayed quiet; he feared saying anything in unison with the others thinking that blending in might make him stand out. The word got around that Jameel slipped in the shower and died as the duty officer that was supposed to be on watch caught a diarrhea spell from the foul chicken at the base the night before. It was fate, a fate that Hashim believed he had created for himself. Nothing would bring him back from how downtrodden he had become. His facade of faith had imploded in him, but he never failed to hide it from the world. His polite demeanor was his new veil, a cloak as impenetrable as the doors of heaven. Hell has never felt as warm. An Unfinished Life.

Acknowledgements

I would like to thank all the ancestors who came before me—my grandfathers and grandmothers, father and mother—for their sacrifices. To my sister and her soul sisters. For the power of the ancients.

To all the poets of Basra, all the MCs from Brooklyn to Babel. For all the words used to express and clear injustices. To all the sisters who are the reason our society is still standing.

To Suheir, Yasiin, Talib, Tariq, Jalaldeen, Lauryn, Andre, Shawn, Christopher and Nasir. Thank you for the codex.

To all those who believe, believed, and will believe. Thank you for your hearts.

To my dear editors at Fernwood and Haymarket, thank you for your patience and belief. To Anthony Arnove, you reached out to me before I knew I could do this and I will forever be grateful.

To my creative friends: keep creating, one day it will all make sense.

To our future generations: time is infinite and short, be in it.

Thank you to you for reading. Let's move as one.

Ameen,
Yassin

Glossary

3ala Rasee, ya gmar—Direct translation: "On my head, my moon" or "Anything for you, my moon."

7afith—Memorizer

Akhi—Brother

Al-Hamdulillah—All praise due to Allah

Allah Yirhamhoom—Allah have mercy on them

Anee moo ibnak—I am not your son

Arrak—An alcoholic beverage made from anise

As-salamu Alaikum—Peace Be Upon You

chai—Tea, not like Chai Latte or Chai Tea, but just tea

Deen—Religion

dijla—Tigris

fitna—Temptation, trial, affliction, distress

Habibi—My love

hub oo iman—Love and faith

hubi—Love

Iqra—Read

Jiddu—Grandfather

klawchi—A con artist

kletcha—A date and pastry desert

Kufr—Sin

la ti3bid—Don't worship

Lek Gawad—Iraqi slang for "you pimp"; derogatory or sarcastic

Maktooba—It was written

Maqam—Traditional Iraqi band

Glossary

Moo'meneen—Believers

Muslimeen—Muslims

Niya—Intent

qozi—Iraq's national dish; a traditional Arab meal made of rice, lamb, and spice

Qurna—The meeting of the Tigris and Euphrates

Sabah Al-Khair—Good morning

Sabah Al-Khara—Shitty morning

Salam—Peace

Shaytan'—The Devil

shbeek—What's wrong?

Sib7a—Prayer beads

Sirat Al-mustaqeem—The straight path

Stakhfarallah—Forgiveness from Allah

Sub7anAllah—Glory to God

Sukr—Sugar

Surat Il-Fil—The Elephant Sura from the Qur'an

tahareeyat—Secret police

Thay3een—Lost

Yallah—C'mon

yil'3an abook labul—God damn your father

Zaatar—Thyme

Zabaaniyah—The Angels of Hell

Zamakan—Space time

Credits

Cover artwork by **Saks Afridi**
Cover type by **Roï Saade**
Cover design by **We Are The Medium**
All writing by **Yassin 'Narcy' Alsalman** (No ghost writer)
Comic book art by **Ashraf Ghori**
Hyena Soldier by **Sedki Al Imam**
Happy Holidays by **Khalid Al Baih**
I Love(d) Baghdad by **Sundus Abdul Hadid**
World War Free Now cover page by **Yassin Alsalman**

Page 6 by **Nahla Tahsin Abdul Jabbar**
Page 19 by **Saks Afridi**
Page 39 by **Nik Brovkin**
Page 20 by **Hala Alsalman**
Page 23, 28, 127 by **Sundus Abdul Hadi**
Page 30, 41 by **Yassin Alsalman**
Page 66, 67 by **The Fakening**
Page 40, 47 by **Alexis Masella for Cartoon Racist**
Page 12, 21, 29, 109 by **Khalid Al Baih**
Page 14 by **Cheb Moha**
Page 124 by **Shams Alsalman**
Page 139 by **Stickerism**
Hashim cover by **Dhimindra Jeevan**

Thank you to **Conseil des arts et des lettres du Québec**
for their generous help in the writing of "Hashim: A Life
Unfinished" through their Vivacité program.

OUR CURRENCY IS EMPATHY.

A SYMPHONY OF SYMPATHY.

About the Author

Real name Yassin Alsalman, Narcy is a musician, director, professor, writer, and actor. He teaches a hip-hop production class and a cultural study of rap and politics at Concordia University. He is the cofounder of WeAreTheMedium, a culture point for publishing, media, and the arts. He currently resides in Tiohtià:k , on unceded Indigenous lands, has his heart in the Arab world, and is grounded on planet Earth. Most importantly, he is a father of two.

About Haymarket Books

Haymarket Books is a radical, independent, nonprofit book publisher based in Chicago.

Our mission is to publish books that contribute to struggles for social and economic justice. We strive to make our books a vibrant and organic part of social movements and the education and development of a critical, engaged, international left.

We take inspiration and courage from our namesakes, the Haymarket martyrs, who gave their lives fighting for a better world. Their 1886 struggle for the eight-hour day– which gave us May Day, the international workers' holiday—reminds workers around the world that ordinary people can organize and struggle for their own liberation. These struggles continue today across the globe—struggles against oppression, exploitation, poverty, and war.

Since our founding in 2001, Haymarket Books has published more than five hundred titles. Radically independent, we seek to drive a wedge into the risk-averse world of corporate book publishing. Our authors include Noam Chomsky, Arundhati Roy, Rebecca Solnit, Angela Y. Davis, Howard Zinn, Amy Goodman, Wallace Shawn, Mike Davis, Winona LaDuke, Ilan Pappé, Richard Wolff, Dave Zirin, Keeanga-Yamahtta Taylor, Nick Turse, Dahr Jamail, David Barsamian, Elizabeth Laird, Amira Hass, Mark Steel, Avi Lewis, Naomi Klein, and Neil Davidson. We are also the trade publishers of the acclaimed Historical Materialism Book Series and of Dispatch Books.

WE ARE THE MEDIUM